THE PRICE OF FREEDOM

THE PRICE OF FREEDOM

A SON'S JOURNEY

Roger A. Mitchell Jr., MD

with Darrius J. Gourdine

Foreword by Roger Mitchell Sr.

Printed in the United States of America
2014 First Edition
10 9 8 7 6 5 4 3 2 1

Subject Index:
Mitchell, Roger Jr. MD
Title: The Price of Freedom: A Son's Journey
1. Memoir   2. Christian   3. Inspirational   4. Forgiveness
5. Service

Paperback ISBN: 978-0-692-25264-2
Ebook ISBN: 978-0-692-27689-1

Edited by Kim A. Rouse, Covenant Consulting LLC:
www.covenantwithyou.com
Co-written by Darrius J. Gourdine, www.artisanblue.com
Cover design by Websignia, LLC, www.websignia.net

The Price of Freedom
www.freedomhasaprice.com

Contents

PRAISE FOR FREEDOM

"Perhaps the greatest obstacle to the fulfillment of one's purpose is the weight of bitterness as a result of life experiences. Few of us realize that the only medication for bitterness is forgiveness and humble service of that which has caused us pain. *The Price of Freedom* shares how these principles liberated Dr. Mitchell toward reconciliation with his own father and fulfillment of his purpose. At the same time, Dr. Mitchell inspires each of us to pay the price of freedom knowing that doing so will allow realization of *your* GOD-ordained purpose."

Rev. Dexter U. Nutall
Pastor – New Bethel Baptist Church
Washington DC

"Wow! *The Price of Freedom A Son's Journey* by Roger A. Mitchell Jr. MD is a must read for the Hip Hop Generation and every teacher who teaches students of color or economically disadvantaged students.

At a time when damaging and pervasive chasms are growing between teachers and students in our urban centers across the county, the Price of Freedom A Son's Journey by Roger A. Mitchell Jr. MD should be required reading to help these educators who feel unprepared to meet the needs of students of color or economically disadvantaged students, and give hope at times of crisis.

I am simply amazed at how this book gives a precise and clear cut way to solving societal issues with lifesaving policy.

At a time when there is a great priority on Black male achievement, this book is an insightful guide to understanding how we can actually break the shackles of fatherlessness, and achieve greatness through service.

Written in a fun yet intellectual manner, Dr. Mitchell has presented some compelling thoughts and has provided a most intriguing perspective on fatherhood in the 21st century and tells us his story with candid transparency and proves that success is not achieved overnight, but can be achieved.

I have read many other books and articles on fatherlessness and find this presentation to be a must-read, and truthful piece of work.

Truly this story of one son's journey towards manhood should be on every father's bookcase in America, it's certainly on mine."

Rev. *Dr. Lennox Yearwood Jr.*
President & CEO
Hip Hop Caucus Education Fund

"*The Price of Freedom* is the remarkable and compelling story of a truly extraordinary man's journey to real freedom. The message is straightforward and much needed today. I commend Dr. Roger Mitchell, Jr. for producing such a significant publication. It is masterful and meaningful.

I am forever grateful to God for sharing Dr. Roger Mitchell, Jr. with me while a member of Agape Family Worship Center. His life has touched mine in so many wonderful ways. I am certain you too will be blessed by reading and embracing the contents of this book. Though the details of your story may differ from his, like Dr. Mitchell, when you sacrifice your anger through forgiveness you can become free—"free to have stronger relationships, free to love, and free to serve."

Lawrence Powell, Senior Pastor
Agape Family Worship Center
Rahway, New Jersey

To my wife Angie, my best friend and life partner. I learn so much from you every day. Nathaniel, Nina, Matthew, and my family, I could not be free to serve without all of your love and support.

To my sisters Donna and Monica, we made it through. Last, but certainly not least, to my Mom, you are truly an angel here on earth.

"A Godly leader finds strength by realizing his weakness, finds authority by being under authority, finds direction by laying down his own plans, finds vision by seeing the needs of others, finds credibility by being an example, finds loyalty by expressing compassion, finds honor by being faithful, finds greatness by being a servant."

- Roy Lessin

FOREWORD

"I was addicted to cocaine to the point where
it was using me more than I was using it."

- Roger Mitchell Sr.

I enlisted in the Army at 17 years old and spent the next 11 years as an Artillery Sergeant. I was part of the USO Tour and traveled all over Europe on weekends with *The Five Gems* singing baritone, with Dennis Edwards on lead. We sang all the hits from *The Temptations, The Four Tops,* and *Marvin Gaye.* I chose not to go to Vietnam because so many of my buddies did not come back, so I returned to my hometown of Elizabeth, New Jersey. I immediately got a job as an insurance claims adjuster with a local agency. A few months later, I got both my real estate and insurance licenses. In no time I was juggling three legitimate hustles straight outta the box!

I thought I was all that and a bag of beans! I was a good-looking, sharp dresser, with a quick-witted tongue and loveable personality. If there were such a thing as "The Community Charismatic Businessman Award" I would have won it several years in a row, hands down. My son Roger often says that I could sell you the shoes off your own feet! I met Roger's mother at my office on a beautiful spring morning. She was an insurance auditor based in Trenton and traveled to our office to make sure we were up to par. I thought she was the finest woman I had seen in a long time. She was not from the area so I asked her out. She said "yes" and we eventually married. A year later, I opened Mitchell Novelties on Chandler Avenue in Newark where I sold costume jewelry, purses, wigs, and other women's accessories. I then bought, Mitchell One-Stop, and parked it on the corner near East Orange High School where I cooked sausages, hamburgers, hotdogs, and sold chips and sodas. It was later converted to a pizzeria in the same neighborhood. These were all good, income-earning businesses. I never kept any of them too long as I would build them up to make a profit and then sell them. I saw other people making money buying and selling one business after the next, so I said to myself, if they can do it, I can too! I never stopped my insurance hustle because it always paid the bills; a reliable source of income. Most of the time I was just bored with one of my businesses so I was always on the hunt for the next hustle.

I found it! My new hustle altered the course of my life for the next ten years. I became the manager of 21 female strippers and escorted them to Larry Holmes' Club in Easton, Pennsylvania. I set up dance programs during the week and on weekends. I paid the girls and they made good tips and I made a nice living. Before I knew it, I was managing 13 male strippers as well. This type of lifestyle kept me out of the house more than any other hustle. I didn't drink when I was managing the strippers because I always wanted to keep a level head. During that time my mother died, and at 42 years old, it was the most devastating thing that ever happened to me. Now, I started drinking and hanging around the bar more often. One night the bartender handed me foil-wrapped cocaine and said "Man take this in the bathroom and do what you got to do." I thought it wasn't going to bother me because I was strong-willed and level headed, so I took it and walked off in my typical confident stride. I was instantly hooked! I started snorting and smoking every chance I got. Cocaine took me from where I was on the ladder of success all the way back down to zero. I lost everything. I left my wife and children because I really believed they loved me so much that they would have allowed me to drag them into using. When I split, Roger Jr. was eight years old.

After being on the streets in Atlantic City for several years I knew I was in a do or die situation. If I had stayed where I was I would have killed myself overdosing. I had a ton of the drug already in my system that could have stopped my heart. I knew all of this stuff at the time, but I was addicted to cocaine to the point where it was using me more than I was using it. I had to run for dear life, so I called Roger Jr.

"Hello."

"Roger... Roger is that you?"

"Dad?"

"Yes son. It's me. I don't have much time. I'm on a pay phone. But I need you to come get me. I need you Roger!"

"Oh my God! Dad! Where are you? Where are you calling me from? Are you OK?" "I'm in Atlantic City. I hit rock bottom but I need to get my life together. This time is gonna be different son. I need help. Can you, can you come get me?"

"Yes, I'll be there as soon as I can."

That day I was serious and I knew that God Himself had intervened on my behalf. When I was walking to the phone booth on New York Avenue in the pouring rain I was fighting back waist-deep water as the ocean flooded the streets. In all my years in Atlantic City that street had never flooded. Right after I hung up the phone with Roger, and began to walk back to my apartment, the water subsided. I immediately felt that I was being totally washed of all the junk that I was in--like I was being baptized right then and there. I fell to my knees and cried like a baby. I knew that my life was about to turn around and God was giving me the chance to start over again.

My son and daughters placed me in an outpatient program at the Washington DC Veterans Administration Hospital. After a few months, they found me a spot in an inpatient program, the Harbor Light Program of the Salvation Army. In six months I received certificates of achievement and was named Chaplain after completing several Bible courses. I pursued the opportunity to help others with their addictions and became a Certified Addiction Counselor (CAC2) and have been counseling people for over 15 years. This book will introduce you to the forgiveness of a son and the thankfulness of his father. I am a proud father of a wonderful son who was there for me and never left my side until he knew that my life was going to be alright. Roger Jr. watched me elevating and moving forward as he was moving forward in medical school. My son is a son that I believe every father would love to have in his corner. I thank God for bringing me through what I had to go through to arrive at this wonderful moment in my life. I've made my peace with my past and with God. My life has been changed and my son and I pray that we are now able to follow in the footsteps and direction of our Lord and Savior Jesus Christ.

For my 75th birthday I was blessed to go to my first baseball game with Roger when he was nearly 40 years old. Every time I looked over at him I had tears in my eyes. What a wonderful feeling to see my son, my best friend and mentor, sitting next to my grandson! I thank you Roger. I thank both of my daughters Monica and Donna; I love you all and thank you for being there for me. I know that I am blessed to be here for you now. I thank everyone who encouraged and taught me to be a better father and a better man. Now that I am teaching at the VA Hospital in Washington DC, it is my sincere prayer to pass this message along to all of my clients. I have a new outlook on life. Every morning I wake up and thank God for my blessings. I usually grab my harmonica and play my favorite tune that sums up my life:

Amazing Grace
How sweet the sound,
That saved a wretch like me.
I once was lost, but now I'm found
Was blind, now I see.

Roger, congratulations on this book. I'm stunned with joy. I love you son.

Roger Mitchell Sr.

Introduction

"Service to others is the rent you
pay for your room here on Earth."

- Muhammad Ali

GROWING up, my mother exposed me to the Civil Rights Movement and Dr. Martin Luther King Jr. Even though he was the only black leader I knew, his life was a great starting point in my journey towards finding my purpose. When I got to high school, I read *The Autobiography of Malcolm X*, which was pivotal to my understanding of the black struggle. I was struck by his confidence and utter boldness in speaking out for the black cause in a time of strife and opposition. Then, in my junior year, I saw the movie *Glory* and it was a total shock to my system. I realized that I did not know a lot about my history. *Shame on me.*

It wasn't until I arrived on the campus of Howard University in the fall of 1992 that I developed an insatiable appetite to consume as much African-American history and literature I could get my hands on. In addition to studying biology, chemistry, and calculus, I spent a lot of time studying African-American history; Comparative Slavery, African Slavery in the Diaspora, and Greco-Roman Slavery. I also read autobiographies and other works of Frederick Douglass, WEB Du Bois, and Booker T. Washington which were more than critical to my intellectual development. What would have happened if WEB Du Bois and Booker T. Washington combined their messages? An explosion of incomparable power and change! I call these two great thinkers the double-headed monster. It is unfortunate that they were at odds with each other and had several different opinions on the same issues.

Through my studies I saw how all those who achieved true freedom had to pay a price for that freedom. Whether it was Booker T. Washington, W.E. B. Du Bois, Marcus Garvey, Martin Luther King Jr., Malcolm X, or Nelson Mandela, all had to pay up through sacrifice; some more than others. I honestly believe that one must give up something in order to truly achieve freedom. In that sacrifice there is a peace and in that peace there is freedom. My story is not novel. Nor does it reveal new principles towards success. What it does, is demonstrate how age-old principles put into practice, will guarantee freedom. This type of freedom sets the stage for a life of success that requires the service of others to be sustainable.

In my case, I was mishandled as child. I carried anger and sadness as a result. When I sacrificed my anger through forgiveness I became free; free to have stronger relationships, free to love, and free to serve. Now that I am in a place of freedom,

serving others keeps me grounded here. I took my fatherlessness and put it on the altar and sacrificed it. Once it was sacrificed, it was gone. Then I realized that in sacrificing, I was still incomplete. As I was moving into the next phase of my life with less baggage, less anger, and less resentment, I had to fill that incomplete missing space with something meaningful; a life of Service. That is why being married was even more critical to my development as I was able to fill it with the love and admiration I have for my wife, along with the covering and provision for my children. I always talk about how critically important it is for a man to have a wife and children.

This book is in response to my seven-minute clip from The Steve Harvey Show in 2012. I was told that someone from my past wanted to thank me. I hate surprises. I had no idea who wanted thank me. I could not believe it when my dad, my best friend, walked out from behind the backstage wall. Ever since then, people have come up to me with similar stories of forgiveness: "After I saw your segment on Steve Harvey, I really listened to what you said about not holding grudges and forgiveness, so I called my dad and now we are on very good terms after several years." Someone else stopped me in church, "I know you don't know me, but my brother has not talked to my father in 10 years and I sent him that clip from Steve Harvey and my father and brother are really talking for the first time! Thank you for that."

Now my life is committed to service. I am free and not worried about the next thing as I stand on service and providing for others. This project coming to fruition has helped many businesses because as much as I am receiving, I am giving. At the end of the day I want readers to understand that service is the most important thing to me. I believe that a lot of people can benefit in their life by filling any void with God. I am truthful with myself in knowing that I am not completely and utterly done being molded into the man God desires me to be. There is this golden thread of Godliness and if you want to know how I forgave my father then you have to know that God played a huge part. I now understand how my continued sacrifice of self through the service of others, particularly, my wife and children, family and church, my community and country, and most importantly God, has made me whole. This sort of sacrifice allows me the ability to maintain such uncompromising freedom. The price each one of us will pay for freedom will be different. What will yours be?

"You can't separate peace from freedom because no one can be at peace unless he has freedom."

- Malcolm X

The contents of this book will lay out what happened throughout my life as a fatherless young man. It shows the type of mindset and steps I took that propelled me into my current position as the Chief Medical Examiner of a large metropolitan area. Please be patient with me, God is not through with me yet. Even though my father was not present due to his crack cocaine abuse, I had all of the necessary ingredients to thrive; a strong, loving, educated mother, a supportive and very successful family, positive male role models, and my faith in Jesus. God showed me that the last piece in my life's puzzle for growth was to forgive my father.

Christmas 1979
One day I will be a doctor!

Chapter One

THE SPLITTING IMAGE

"What you leave behind is not what is engraved in
stone monuments, but what is woven into the lives of others."
-Pericles

I grew up in a middle class community in South Orange, New
Jersey. I was born into a two parent home with two older sisters.
Since my dad and I were the only males in the house, his presence
was crucial to me from birth until the age of eight years old. Every
morning when I woke up he was there and every night when I went
to bed he was there. Dad in the house, going to work, or taking
me along with him was all I had ever known. When he left I was
devastated. I often overheard adult conversations about my dad and
drugs. *Drugs? What the heck were drugs to an eight-year old New Jersey
kid from the suburbs?*

At an early age, I was a staple in my dad's daily routines. Whether
he took me to work with him at the insurance company or if he was
working on the Cordoba in the driveway, he was just a few feet away,
and I was his willing side-kick. Even if I did nothing more than
hand him a wrench, his smile of encouragement meant the world
to me. He often graced me with a thumbs up, followed by "Good
job!" My dad was the kind of man that was loved everywhere he
went. He knew everyone, which kept me grinning from ear-to-ear
just to be seen with him. When he entered a room it felt like life
stopped because "Mitch" was here. No one called him Roger. He

was "Mitch-the-Main-Man." Menial tasks like going to the corner store became major outings for me because I was Mitch's boy. When we strolled together, him with a big bop and me with a little bop, it was as if we both heard Shaft's theme music playing in the background. Ask anyone who remembers him, he was straight-up cool!

Dad created a loving home environment and I had a great deal of respect for both of my parents. Up until the age of seven, things were normal in the Mitchell house. My dad displayed his affection for his wife and children regularly. This loving environment was all I knew and my community was a collection of similar nuclear families. Saturday mornings were particularly special to me. It meant four things: Cheerios, Woody Woodpecker, a slew of Kung-Fu movies on Channel Five, and riding with my dad to the bank on Broad Street in Newark. I liked going to the bank with him to conduct transactions from all of his businesses. It made me feel important and the tellers always gave me candy. At my age, this trip was more than a weekly routine—it was an adventure! Since we traveled the same route each time, the neighborhood McDonald's always stood out in my mind. To this day, I get flashbacks to Saturday mornings with dad every time I see those golden arches. Sometimes we would sneak off and get pancakes at The Hamburger House on Central Avenue and Halsted. It's no longer there and has been replaced by a Dunkin' Donuts and Baskin Robbins. That spot will always be The Hamburger House to me. This was 1981 and The Hamburger House was black-owned and operated. What a great feeling seeing black men cooking, serving, and having a good time. It was almost like going to the barbershop without getting a haircut. Most of the time, when we went there mom never knew. "It's just between the boys," dad would say, winking and giving me a look of confidence. We both laughed at our secret. It was our Saturday morning experiences that truly bonded me to my dad. Those days are actually the best memories I have from my childhood.

> There is nothing more important than a father being willing to spend time with his son. That quality time will influence a boy's growth and maturity just knowing there is a consistent male figure in his life.

It wasn't so much that my dad threw me a football or sat and played video games with me. Nor was he the kind of father who took me fishing, or came to any soccer games. I never saw him in the audience when I played the Scarecrow in The Wizard of Oz in high school. What bonded me with him was his constant presence. I loved the simple fact that he was physically there—Old Spice and all. I cherished the notion of coming home; hearing his voice, seeing and smelling him. Since I don't have biological brothers, and my sisters are both older than me by at least six years, my dad occupied a position that I never knew could become vacant. I never imagined what the critical requirement of a "present" father in a young boy's life would play. Feeling his vacancy was more than I could bear.

"Word is bond!"

I loved hip-hop growing up. LL Cool J, Run D MC, and Cool Moe Dee were among my favorites. My friends and I felt cool when we spoke to each other and used the popular catchphrase, "Word is bond!" This meant that your words had meaning. So if I said something, I meant it. I know most young guys have heard this saying or used it, and when I was coming up I originally learned it from hip hop songs. There's something special to a young boy when his dad makes a decision and articulates it. Like that strong masculine confidence in a man's voice when he puts his foot down. You know the one when your dad gives you that look and said, "Alright, that's enough!" You also knew playtime was over when you were jumping on the bed and it was past bedtime and he said, "OK, lights out!

Go to bed!" My dad's words meant everything to me. They helped to frame me even at that age. My older sisters laughed at me when I tried to declare something in the house trying to mimic my dad; never mind the fact that I was the youngest person in the house. After all, I was going to be a man eventually, so why not start now? My dad was awesome in my eyes. I wanted to be just like him when I grew up. I wanted to put on his shoes, his necktie, and sit at the head of the table like he did. More important, I wanted to have an office to go to like he did.

The words of a good dad mean everything to any young boy.

The earliest recollection that I have of things going south was when I was around eight years old. I started hearing my parents argue often. This was very unusual to me. I had never been privy to shouting matches before in my home nor with any of my other family members. My father's voice had changed. The voice of authority that I had grown used to, now spoke cruel words to my mother. For the first time, I noticed holes in the walls in the kitchen next to the sink. Holes that were created by my dad's fists as his arguments with my mother obviously grew more frustrating for him. It is understandable how an eight-year-old child, who revered his dad up to this point, was in a state of total confusion. I quickly stepped into the role as the man of the house because I was called upon to console my older sisters. None of us was could have anticipated this change in our home. The paradigm shifted and I had to mature quickly and accept the role of comforter even though I was far too young to accurately comprehend it. All I was able to do at that stage was to go with the flow and try to make sense out of what ultimately made no sense to me.

> "The most important question in the world is,
> why is the child crying?"
>
> *- Alice Walker*

Everything I had considered important changed that year. I began to see my dad through very different eyes. I was a reluctant witness to all that happened around me. For reasons I did not know or understand then, my dad left. My father finally moved out and my life was never the same. For him, it may have been a sense of relief. It may have been a freedom that he had not experienced in a long time. I'm not sure. Whatever he was feeling, that sentiment did not resonate with me. My daddy was gone. Even though I still saw him around the neighborhood I didn't see him.

Compared to the other kids, I believe I was a pretty normal boy who enjoyed going outside in the summer riding my yellow and black BMX with yellow mag wheels around Hamilton Road. My most vivid memory of riding that bike was doing jumps and tricks off the "pipe-jump" into the street. Like most boys my age, I was heavy into sports and enjoyed playing and watching football, basketball and baseball. I gravitated toward soccer because it was one of the most successful and visible sports in my town. It was fun, easy to learn, and I played it all year around from ages 7-13. Besides, I was really good at it!

BROKEN PROMISES

> "Promises are like crying babies in a theater,
> they should be carried out at once."
>
> *- Norman Vincent Peale*

The level of respect that I had for my dad quickly diminished. In an instant, what took eight years to build only took one year to destroy. Eight years of admiration was lost because of one year of broken promises. What a difficult year. Of course I didn't understand the impact of my dad leaving and how it would impact me later in life, but even in not understanding, his absence felt like a one-hundred pound weight crushing my heart. As an adult with full control of my articulation, it would be easy to explain my hurts, fears, frustrations or challenges. If someone were to ask me how I felt during that time, I don't know if I would have had the proper words to describe it. I remember telling my oldest sister, "Don't worry, things are going to be OK," when I had no clue as to whether they would be. I remember my mother carrying me to my room when I fell asleep on the sofa watching Fantasy Island, trying to stay awake when my dad arrived home from work—only to be disappointed that the arrivals became later and later and sometimes not at all. In retrospect, the strain on my parents' relationship was evident. My father chose the nightlife over helping me with my homework. Drinking and clubbing were much more important than my soccer games and school projects. Even the expression on my father's face changed. He was no longer able to look me in the eye with a smile and a message of encouragement. As he changed I also changed. This was too much for an eight year old to bear, yet I was forced to deal with it.

Although my mother and sisters were always there, I felt alone; like no one understood what I was going through. I disconnected from my emotions and connected with activities at school and organized sports. Soccer went from being a pastime to a passion. My focus on improving my game was more about taking my mind off what was going on at home. When I ran full speed during the games, I didn't think about my father's absence. I practiced hard and wanted to be the best. Who knows? Being the best may bring my dad back.

Not only did he leave, but now he was breaking promises. He went from being the dad who took his son to the bank every Saturday and secret trips to The Hamburger House, to the dad who said he would be there to see me play soccer and not show up. I don't believe there is anything more devastating to a child than the broken promise of a respected adult, especially a parent.

There is no greater pain than a boy being let down by his father.

Over the next two years, my level of respect, my expectations, and my hope in my father were at an all-time low. Whether it was during the holidays when he would con me out of my Christmas money that Grandpa Buddy gave me, saying, "I just need to borrow a couple of dollars son, I will give it back" or not showing up for holidays, each disappointment led to more disappointment. This became my life. I cannot count the number of times I looked to the sidelines and found a vacant spot where my father should have been standing when I played soccer. Playing without my father there to support me deeply hurt. I was a very good player and I celebrated with my teammates and their families, but never with my dad. All of my Jewish friends' dads were at the games. As part of the Cougar Teams of South Orange and Maplewood we were known for our exceptional skills and sportsmanship. My team was one of the best travelling teams in the State of New Jersey for our age bracket and I was a starter. All of my sporting accomplishments were applauded by my coaches. I got pats on the back from my mom and the rest of my family. Our team even made it to the newspaper for being undefeated. Dad really should've been there.

Looking back, I think about how funny it was those times when he kept his promise. He'd pick me up and take me to a girlfriend's house and plop me in front of a TV with some snacks. He would go into the back room with the woman and stay for several hours. Then when he came out, he shook the dust off and drove me home in silence. In the past, when he lived with us, there was constant conversation in the car, "Roger look at this…, Roger look over there…" There was nothing but instruction the whole ride. When I drive around with my kids now, I always talk about things in passing and do my best to put the world around them in the proper context.

Each disappointment stung worse for every broken promise. I tried to forget the last time dad let me down as to reassure myself that the next time would be different. This didn't work because he let me down again and again. Imagine, I actually believed him when he told me that he would pick me up or attend a game. I still can't believe all those times I sat on the front porch waiting or looking at the sidelines. Dad was a no-show. Same result, different day.

SINK OR SWIM

I learned how to swim at seven years old on July 4th at my Uncle Joe's house in Piscataway. Every Christmas and 4th of July our family gathered at Uncle Joe's and my dad's sister, Aunt Joan's house. Everyone in my family were big swimmers except me. When my dad taught me to swim, he just grabbed me and threw me in the deep end. My mom was terrified. "Mitch what are you doing?" My father coached me and said I could do it, but I wasn't sure. I was scared. I remember hitting the bottom and slowly rising to the top. I could hear him yelling, "Swim to me Roger! Swim to me!" I doggie-paddled toward him. I didn't even know I could do such a thing! I realized that I was making headway when I heard my entire family cheering, "You can do it Roger, you can do it Roger!" With my family still cheering in the background I gained momentum and made it safely to the side.

The ones who really love you will always challenge you to be your best even if you feel uncertain. A father will know when his son is ready even if his son doesn't.

Chapter Two

KODAK MOMENT

"If you have no confidence in self,
you are twice defeated in the race of life."

- Marcus Garvey

OVER the next couple of years, dad moved from place-to-place. I often thought, *I'm more stable as a ten year old than he is as a grown man.* He's 35 years older than me, so I expected a lot more from an *old* person. He finally moved to Rochester, New York with one of his many girlfriends. I remember a particular visit to Rochester that changed my life and my opinion of my father to an even lower level than it had already been. **July 4, 1984** is etched into my memory forever. When I look back, I liken it to my Kodak moment. Dad invited me to his house for the entire week. Mom was leery in sending me but she never wanted to interfere with our relationship. She heard that dad was getting better so she wanted to be supportive. I insisted on going.

"Roger I don't know if this is such a good idea."

"I'll be fine. I'll be careful and if anything happens I will call you. I promise."

"Well OK."

I imagine she spoke with my dad behind the scenes, but I did not have any knowledge of that. She probably said to him, "Mitch, don't mess this up." She put me on a $50 flight from Newark to Rochester and I could not have been happier. Dad picked me up

from the airport and the weekend was off to a great start. We spent
the holiday at the home of a childhood friend with a nice pool. The
barbeque was tasty and I could not remember the last time I had
so much fun with my dad. All I kept thinking was, this is the type
of life I am supposed to be sharing with him. I loved it! I was sure
that he loved it too! Then the small disappointments started to rear
their ugly heads again. He started leaving me alone in the house for
a few hours and then return late in the evening. He left me with a
house full of food and $20 or more dollars on the table each day.
This went on a few times and then it happened. I remember it like
it was yesterday.

On July 7th we were cruising back to his house in his new, baby
blue Pontiac Grand AM. Prior to the Grand AM, he had a Nova,
Mailbu, Cordoba, Roadster and Riviera. He was always in front of
the latest car craze and this car was a sight to see! It was a warm
evening and the sun was just setting. We pulled into the driveway
and he turned the radio down just as I was learning the words to
"Roxanne Roxanne."

"Go on in the house. I'll be right back." He said in a hurried
tone.

I immediately thought of the disappointing moments when he
said things like this and never kept his word. I felt uneasy in the pit
of my stomach. This time he may have been telling the truth so I
had to take his word.

"Where you goin' dad?"

"I'm gonna put gas in the car, we have a long week ahead and I
need to make sure we're gassed up."

"Well can I go with you?"

"No, no, just go inside and put some Ravioli on the stove. You
must be hungry, it's been a long drive today."

I gave him a worried look so he tried to reassure me.

"I'll be right back."

He then flashed his thousand-watt smile and patted my head. It
was that familiar smile which used to bring me comfort and warmth

years earlier. Even though it was a bit foreign to me now since I hadn't felt that warmth in a long while, I liked it. I didn't push the issue because I was just happy to be in Rochester with him for what was turning out to be one of our best times together. I decided to get out of the car with my mind focused on Ravioli. He popped the trunk and I took my bags out. I closed the trunk and stood next to the car as I watched him back out of the driveway. I waved and he waved back. Beep! Beep! He sped off.

I entered the house and found the can of Ravioli. I put it in a pot, turned on the stove and then went into the living room to turn on the TV. I ate the Ravioli and even washed the pot. I waited in sheer anticipation for the exact moment when I would either hear the car pull up in the driveway or hear the keys opening the door. Neither sound came for the next five hours, so I changed into my pajamas and put myself to bed.

I woke up the next morning wondering if dad ever came home. I went to his room and his bed had not been slept in. I didn't know what to do or think. I paced the hallway with my hands on my head trying to figure out my next move. This was far too much pressure for a ten year old but this was my life. Should I call mom or try to find dad? Should I eat something? Should I go back to sleep and hope when I wake up he would be home? Maybe it's just too early. Should I look out the window toward the driveway for the nine- teenth time? Should I make enough Ravioli for lunch for the both of us?" Question after question raced through my mind. Wait, did I just hear his keys? Should I walk to the corner to see if his car is approaching? Should I call a neighbor? Should I, Should I, Should I...

I sat and waited more than nine hours. Still no dad.

The house was silent that day. Although the TV was on with The Dukes of Hazzard, the house felt eerily quiet. I had to break the silence by speaking out loud. This may sound crazy, but sit in an empty room for over nine hours and I guarantee you will start speaking aloud. It's a common human reaction. Human beings are designed by God for companionship, "It is not good for man to be alone" (Gen. 2:18). I began to speak to my dad as if he were there. I threw out questions that I knew would not be answered. I said things to invoke a smile knowing that the smile would never be seen. I told him about my last soccer game and my recent part in a school play. That night was even quieter than the day. Every creek in the house seemed to be magnified. Every cricket was on full surround sound. I decided to do the big boy thing and get myself ready for bed again. I ate my Ravioli alone. I washed, turned off the TV and got into bed. I laid in the magnified silence of house creeks and crickets until my eyes became heavy and the questions in my head ceased.

The second day came and went with the same outcome. No dad. Although I had developed somewhat of an uncertainty in moving forward, I was getting used to the routine of taking care of myself. The questions from day one resurfaced in my head. "Should I... Should I... Should I... Should I check the driveway for the one hundred and nineteenth time?" I remember making gut-wrenching screams at the top of my lungs: "When are you coming home? What am I supposed to do? Why aren't you here?" The tears gushed down my face and my Luke Skywalker t-shirt was drenched. I flashbacked to a conversation I overheard between my mother and sister saying that they thought my dad was addicted to drugs. At the time, I said to myself, there is no way he could be addicted. Day two was over. Ravioli and bedtime.

I woke up with a plan. Day three was going to be different. I had my dad's business card so I made a few calls to his office. I was repeatedly told by the receptionist that he wasn't in the office yet. Over the past two years I became a very independent child because I had to do a lot of things on my own. My mom gave me a couple hundred dollars, so I decided to call a cab. I also had money from earlier in the week when my dad threw $20 on the table the first few days of my visit and said he was going to "work." Calling a cab was bold for a ten year old but I didn't know what else to do. I was a very confident child. Back home, I frequently had taken matters into my own hands as I became man of the house to my mom and two sisters. I was more afraid of the disappointment of whatever my dad would tell me, than calling a cab and being driven somewhere. The cab pulled up in the exact spot I wished my dad's car would have. I calmly got in and handed the driver the business card and told him this was the address where I needed to be taken. I looked out the window for most of the ride and the varying green shades of beeches, elms and maples, along the roads in Rochester merged together in slow motion. I now had a myriad of new questions running through my mind. No longer was my head filled with the "Should I" questions. My thoughts were now directed at questions for my dad. "Where were you? Are you OK? Are you ever coming home? What do you want me to do? Do you want me to go back to New Jersey? Why are you too busy for me? Do you even love me?"

We pulled into the parking lot of dad's job. I paid the cab driver and asked him to wait for me. He said he would. I got out and calmly walked inside the building. I had never been to his job in Rochester so this was both an exploratory and a curiosity visit. Although I had called numerous times, I had to see for myself that my dad had not been to his office. Barely able to see over the receptionist's desk, I asked her if she could show me to my father's office. I will never forget the incredulous look on her face when I told her who I was. Her first thought must have been why I was there without an adult. She walked me into my father's office to prove to me that he wasn't there. She was a very polite woman and I'm sure she felt bad for me. Not knowing where my dad actually was left her almost as helpless as I was. Although I didn't feel helpless at the time, I was 10 years old in a city hours away from my home in New Jersey. I just didn't know what or how to feel. All I knew for sure was that the knot in my stomach and the aches throughout my body were real and I did not feel good. I had been abandoned for three days so far and didn't know how much longer it would be. I had learned to be responsible and to take care of myself, yet this was a dangerous situation my dad placed me in. My lack of fear and self-confidence could be attributed to God whom at that time I did not know. However, I felt a spiritual force was definitely present.

I entered dad's office and looked around. It was a simple office: a mahogany desk, a brown pleather chair, a grey typewriter, a beige file cabinet, and a beige phone. He had a window that overlooked the parking lot. There were even pictures of my sisters pinned to a cork board. I stood there gazing at all of the equipment needed to have a productive office. Everything was there—except dad. Where was he? I thanked the receptionist for showing me his office and I could once again see the sorrow in her eyes. She walked me to the cab to make certain I was OK and would be returned safely. The driver assured her and I was driven back to the empty house.

When I walked in the front door my routine was different. No longer was I looking out the window for his car. No longer was I listening attentively for the sound of his keys opening the door. Instead, I was packing to go home. My thoughts had changed from wondering where dad was, to wondering what I was going to tell my mom. The transition of dad leaving was now complete in both my head and heart. When dad moved out of our home, my heart became devoid of him. With this trip and the series of events that took place, dad was totally erased from my heart. How could someone who claims to love me engage in such a selfish act on his own child? As much as it hurt, I still did not understand the full impact of the situation he placed me in. I was left alone to fend for myself without the luxuries that kids have today: internet, Facebook or social media. I could not text message someone to rescue me. There were no cell phones back then. I truly was on my own; yet I was confident and determined to make sound decisions at my young age. Calling home to alert my mother was the next decision I had to make.

"Hi mom."

"Hi Roger! How are things going there with you and daddy? Are you having a good time?"

"No. I'm not feeling well and I want to come home. Dad has been working nonstop and I just want to come home." I didn't want to tell my mother the truth. I didn't want her to panic. I couldn't imagine the trauma of her knowing that dad had left me alone for three days. I don't know how she would have reacted if I had told her, but I didn't want to find out.

"What! What's the matter? Are you very sick? Put your father on the phone!"

"Dad is not here right now. I just need for you to buy me a plane ticket. I want to come home."

After that conversation, mom made the arrangements to get me home. I'm sure she had a lot of questions ready and waiting for me upon my return. I prepared myself for that. I'm sure she had some words for my dad. I doubt he would have cared. I spent the rest of the afternoon in front of the television as I awaited my departure from dad's house. I would not be able to fly out until early the following morning so I had another day of boredom. I sat alone with my many thoughts. I no longer spoke to my dad out loud as I had nothing more to say.

The irony is that on the final day of my shortened vacation with him, he showed up that evening. I heard the car pull in the driveway and then the keys opening the door; the two sounds I had been longing for finally came at a time when I no longer cared to hear them. He was in a state of intoxication as I can still remember him breathing over me as I lay motionless in bed. He stumbled out, went into his room, and passed out on his bed face down. The next morning I woke my dad up at 5 AM to tell him that I was leaving. For the first time in four days, I walked into my father's bedroom and there was a body lying in the bed. He was sound asleep from four nights of partying. I shook him hard a few times until he woke up. He looked at me confused. I don't know if he was confused as to why I woke him up or confused as to who I was. Clearly, he was not the cool coherent "Mitch-the-Man" I had known him to be. I saw a very different man. This was no longer the man that I grew to admire for simply being there. He no longer warmed my heart. It was also the first time I saw him cry. Similar to how I was crying out for him a few days before.

"I need you Roger," he said all choked up. "You can't leave!"

"I can't be with you. I can't until you get some help."

"Son, I'm going to get some help soon."

"Well until you get some help, I can't be around you!"

I stood in the doorway glaring at him and breathing heavily. My emotions were in overdrive. My dad no longer looked at me lovingly. Instead, it was an old, tired, and depleted stare. The man lying in bed was a sick and I knew I couldn't help him.

"Dad, I'm going home. I promise if I could help you I would. But I can't. Goodbye."

I turned away and walked to the front door as I heard the cab approaching the driveway. I walked out to the cab dragging my bag. It was dark at 5 AM so the driver had a light on in the cab to look down at his papers. He glanced through his mirror and saw me coming and popped the trunk. I walked back into the house and he stepped out of the cab and moved toward the back of the trunk. I came out with another bag and he took it and loaded it on top of my first bag. I went back in and came out with another bag. He took it as well.

"Is that it?"

"Yeah," I said out of breath.

My dad never appeared in the doorway or window to see me off.

The driver kept looking at the back door of the driveway as if he was waiting for an adult to appear. He stared at me like, who is this kid? Where are his parents?

"You're going to the airport right?"

"Yes, to the airport please."

When I arrived home, things were never the same. The fact that my friends came from solid families with both parents in the home became magnified. I felt like I was an outsider looking in on the lives of my friends who still had their fathers. I had this vision of being on one side of a fence and my complete family was on the other side.

My family unit was broken and I was forced to become the man of the house before I realized what that truly meant. Nevertheless, I did what I saw other dads do in their homes. Each act of "manhood" that I performed was done because I thought it was right. The fact remained, however, that I was only a child and needed someone to teach me the very things I took upon myself to do. It bothered me that I had no frame of reference as to what drugs were. I gradually came to the understanding that drugs were bad. Drugs meant you leave your family and run around with other women. Drugs meant you leave your 10-year-old son alone for three days. Drugs make you steal from your children. When I returned home I did not tell my mother everything. I just told her that she was right about dad being on drugs. I told her that I didn't think his house was the right place for me and I just needed to come home. She never pressed me for any more information.

My time in Rochester was a very traumatic experience that set my life on its my current trajectory. In my neighborhood the families consisted of blacks and Jews. So at 10 years old this was my bar mitzvah—my rite of passage into manhood. Although traumatic, my experience was not as bad as the rites of passage in other cultures where the parents set the young boy out on an island with a spear and say get back home the best way you can. If the boy made it back home he was worthy to be called a man. If he didn't, he was unworthy. I made it back home. In retrospect, I think back to that July 4th at Uncle Joe's pool where my dad threw me into the deep end. I knew it was a matter of life or death. I stepped out on the edge to go find my dad at work that day. When he wasn't there, I knew I had to swim.

I am still amazed at how God orchestrated my life without me having a clue. Only God could provide me with two traumatic events on July 4th weekend at the ages of 7 and 10 that set me on a trajectory that forever changed my life. As America celebrates its independence; its freedom every 4th of July, I too have made my life-long work of celebrating the freedom and liberty of forgiveness. Isn't God amazing?

Every couple of years after my Rochester visit, my dad would call or show up for a minute and then disappear. Each time he made promises to get help and each time I made promises to help him. Little did I know that of all our promises spoken to each other would be kept by both of us twelve years later.

Chains are broken over time. There is a stretch and a pull and then a stretch and a pull....until snap! You are FREE!

Chapter Three

VILLAGE TO MANHOOD

"Manhood is taking care of your family and
being able to bless other people..."

- Magic Johnson

IN the midst of the turmoil of my life, God blessed me with a great
group of friends who had stable fathers in their homes. Being
accepted by my peers had become as important to me as the acceptance of my father. When my friends' families welcomed me into
their homes, I happily embraced them. My best friend was Talmage
Thompson. I met him when I was about seven. He and his family
lived two doors down from me. Talmage and I were inseparable. He
had two parents in his home in addition to two brothers and a sister.
This nuclear family became a second family to me as Mr. Thompson
filled a void that my father left vacant. My mom worked late so I
was at their house nearly every day. My mother trusted the family
and was happy that I had a positive male role model in my life. I
recall when I came back from Rochester upset about my vacation
and Mrs. Thompson explained to me what was going on with my
dad. Everyone knew Mitch was a "baller" and what he was involved
with. I appreciated her talk, and with a better understanding of what
was going on with my dad, I kept my emotions about him bottled
up inside.

Real manhood is the ability to provide and protect. A real man will provide for his wife, his children, and his loved ones. There are a variety of levels to provision and it isn't simply financial.

Despite the disappointment, loneliness and despair, I felt love and acceptance in the Thompson home. "Pop Thompson" as he was affectionately known, showed me something valuable that I had never seen before; a father praying in a circle with his wife and children. This example of faith and love changed my life. Pop Thompson prayed for everything! He prayed before each meal. He prayed before we left for church. He prayed after we came home from church. He prayed when we went to a football game. He left prayers and inspirational quotes throughout the house: on the bathroom mirror, closet doors, kitchen cabinets, walls—wherever there was a smooth surface. I had never been exposed to such consistent encouragement and faith. Pop Thompson made time for his three boys, and he spent quality time with his daughter. If the Thompson family had an activity, I was invited to attend as they never made me feel like a neighbor or outsider. With every invitation, it grew increasingly more obvious that the theme of their activities were: seek faith and seek family. This theme stayed with me through my teenage years and helped shape my thought processes as I began my journey into manhood.

Each time I visited the Thompson's, countless lessons were imparted to me. Pop Thompson taught me that a man can be responsible, that he can be reliable and dependable. I learned that follow-through was possible and that promises could be kept. This was invaluable to me as I had made a promise to my father that I had no idea if I could fulfill. Pop Thompson showed me strength and security at the same time. He led the type of family I wanted, yet I never felt envious or jealous of his children. Mrs. Thompson was also very special to me. She gave me and her three son's haircuts. I got my first shag down to my neck, and later on a v-neck in the back to compliment my Gumbie. Talmage inherited his mother's skills and started cutting hair in his basement in high school. He recently celebrated his 14th year owning the GTI Square Barber Shop in East Orange, not far from the original site of my beloved Hamburger House.

Mentors help young people navigate and interpret life lessons. Whether that mentor is in the form of family, friends, a coach or a counselor, having a consistent caring adult in the life of a young person may arguably be the single most important predictor of success.

I am thankful to Pop Thompson for giving me something that I desperately needed. My family wasn't poor. We had enough money for food, household expenses, and vacations. I never wanted for any of those things. What I lacked was an emotional currency. In my house we didn't have emotional extras—there wasn't enough to go around nor was there ever seconds. I was searching for an emotional deposit and I needed someone to pour into me. I needed someone to show me what manhood looked like; manhood that included character, integrity, discipline and maturity. It was at this time that I was given the most important deposit I have ever received in my life. I was told by Pop Thompson that what I needed from my natural father could be found in a spiritual Father. What I had been seeking, I already had. I just simply wasn't aware.

A father to the fatherless…
is God in his holy dwelling.

                                    -Psalm 68:5

The events that I experienced up to this moment allowed me to recognize the missing piece to my personal puzzle. By witnessing a missing father and a present father, I found a perfect Father. Once I came into the knowledge of God as a Father, I began speaking outwardly to Him as I had once spoken outwardly to my now absent dad. Now I had a surrogate when I spoke aloud so there was a strong element of confidence. My Father is omnipresent—He's everywhere at the same time. My Father is omnipotent—He can do all things. I talked to God whenever I had questions and it made me feel better. If I was feeling bad or something was going on that I did not understand, I went into my room and talked it over with God. I talked to God more than I talked to my mother.

One Sunday I was sitting in church and the pastor asked if anyone wanted to get baptized and join the church. I got up and walked down the aisle. My mom gave me a look like, "What are you doing?" I didn't turn to ask her for permission or if this was something she thought I should do. I walked up to the pulpit with confidence and gave my life up. My relationship with Him was so intimate. I was totally in my own head most of the time. Even when I was acting out on stage or as Student Council President in sixth and seventh grade, my true self was inside my head, and it still is today. This was the earliest foundation that spirituality played in my life. It transformed what was a very difficult time for me into an environment that I could manage. It helped ground and prepare me for the father I would one day become. God as my Father gave me a true sense of what a dad is supposed to be, because I had one with superpowers all along. Now that I was fully engaged with Him, I knew that He could teach me what to do when I became a father.

We grew up in a Christian household. As I think back to Friday nights at Bible study in church, mom set the much needed foundation for my growth through the consistent example she was providing. While the adults were having Bible study upstairs, the kids were in the basement playing or watching TV. Before it was over, the members would pray over all of the children. We were all getting indoctrinated into what God had for us at an early age. Mom's diligent search for God was one of the reasons my dad had to leave the house. As my dad was pursuing exploits in his night life, my mother was searching for the truth in Christ.

Being introduced to God and becoming a Godly young man was not easy nor did it occur overnight. I still had a lot to learn and made numerous mistakes. But I had living examples. I had uncles who showed me the benefit of hard work. I had teachers and coaches who were willing to give an encouraging word. I had great mentors like Pop Thompson, my uncles, my mom, aunts and countless others who poured into me on a regular basis by showing me the benefits of making the right choices. That's why I am so passionate about our youth and gun violence. When I am speaking in urban communities I urge them to stop applauding the use of violence as the primary means of conflict resolution. My job is to encourage them to define success by integrity, character, discipline, hard work and commitment.

Modeling behavior is how children learn to interact with their environment. It is through witnessing the actions of others that they learn what is acceptable. So when a community defines success by the acquisition of material things; cars, clothing and jewelry, so will the young person standing witness.

My Uncle Joe taught me what a husband looked like. He showed me what it meant to be the patriarch of the family by bringing everyone together. He was very successful in his career and was the Assistant Commissioner at the Department for Banking and Insurance for the State of New Jersey. He smoked a pipe and had a hearty laugh. He had phenomenal strength and was a star football player in high school. Sadly, he did not see me graduate from medical school because he died from complication of diabetes. He was instrumental to my life on so many levels. At times when I was struggling in college and did not want to call my mother to ask for money, I called Uncle Joe. Without hesitation, he sent me a couple hundred dollars.

With my dad gone, my mother stepped in and became the model of success. After a bitter divorce and being left to raise three children by herself, my mother could have easily played the role of the victim. Instead, she exemplified success. She never wavered. She never allowed me to feel inadequate or display a sense of lack. She never allowed me to feel sorry for myself because she certainly didn't feel sorry for herself. She understood that success is judged on character and not on driving a Maybach. She held her head high in the midst of turmoil and taught my sisters and me valuable lessons in doing so. I learned that life throws you curve balls when you expected a fastball, but you still have an opportunity to succeed and hit a grand slam homerun.

I was a latch-key kid. When I came home from school, I completed my homework and prepared the evening meal for my family. I felt proud giving my mother a home-cooked meal after a long day at work. I often made baked chicken and seasoned it with salt and pepper with a little butter underneath the skin. I put it in the oven on 350 degrees for about 45 minutes. I also learned how to flash broil the chicken because I liked it crispy. I made Uncle Ben's rice when rice boxes had the aluminum spout. It took me a while to learn how to make it perfectly, but I finally got it. Then I boiled the frozen block vegetables of either succotash or corn. Mom always provided good instructions and told me to put a little water with salt in the bottom of the pot and place the frozen block into the water.

She told me that it's done when the block falls off and the vegetables begin to steam. Whenever my sister Monica came home I wanted to impress her also. After she and mom tasted my cooking they usually smiled and said, "It's so good!" Chicken, vegetables and rice were my staples. Thank you mom for showing me the true meaning of mentorship and living your life as a constant role model.

When I coupled the faith lessons I had newly learned with a real example of success and mentorship, I started to become the teenager that could withstand anything. Many of the nuggets of wisdom I drop on young men today were obtained during this stage of my development. I can clearly remember examples that encourage the way I think today.

It is so important to instill values in the minds of our young men. Values come from anyone or anything that appears to be a model of success or manhood. A young man learns what success looks like from his friends, the 'streets,' the media, or at home.

Chapter Four

TACKLING OPPOSITION

"Too much on my mind
Just too much on my mind…"

-Leaders of the New School

AS my journey into manhood continued, my mother informed me that we would be relocating to Princeton. This meant that I would be moving from my childhood home and entering a new high school in the middle of my freshman year. I had already gained friends and classmates who were matriculating together, but now I would be attending a different school not knowing anyone. Although thoughts of fear and uncertainty naturally entered my mind, my resolve became absolute when I thought of the strength and example my mother emulated. I wanted to be strong and not add to the weight of the move so I squashed my fear and accepted the transition with my head held high. Neither of us were prepared for the oppositions and obstacles we soon faced. Regardless, my mother had become the family rock and was the essence of strength. She stood and fought battles that only a father should have to fight. As I watched her confront these challenges head on, it taught me the proper attitude to have when I faced my own challenges. Whether it was the long commute from her job in Trenton to our old house in South Orange or the preparation and research required for buying a new house, my mother handled it.

I was one of a small number of African-American students in

high school. I was in an even smaller number of African-American students who were interested in pre-medicine which focused on the study of science and math. These subjects always intrigued me and I thought of pursuing the study of science in college someday. I would never have imagined that I would receive opposition from the very people who were supposed to encourage and support the pursuit of my dreams. Without explanation, the high school administration did not feel I was adequately prepared to excel in higher level classes. They placed me in basic math and science, and suggested that the curriculum would be too difficult for me. I had many things working for me that told me otherwise. I was enrolled in advance science and math classes in my previous high school, I had a strong belief in God, and a mother who had become the epitome of strength. There was no way we were going to back down.

Opposition from school became a pivotal moment in my life. It taught me how to navigate conflict and how to assert my God-given power. My mother, the daughter of a nurse and physician, knew she had power. She knew that her children were heirs to something great in this country and she stood as my advocate. This was not the first time that there was an attempt to label me in the class room. I recall in third grade, I was labeled as disruptive and pulled out of class without my mother's knowledge and placed in a remedial class. My mother became aware of this and consented to have me tested for the Intelligent Quotient Test (IQ). I was seated in a small room with a thinly-built white man with a red tie, white shirt, and black sweater vest. He was mild- mannered, soft-spoken, and very reassuring as he provided directions. I completed a written test, read passages aloud, and placed round and square pegs in their proper holes. He also showed me several ink blot images and appeared astounded by my answers. The end result suggested my IQ score was much higher than normal for my age. Consequently, now my elementary school district wanted to promote me two grades ahead!

I don't blame the school administration as they were only being led by what they were conditioned to believe. Unfortunately, it is widely presumed that African-Americans could only obtain true success in athletics or entertainment. Of course there have been exceptions to the rule. Equally important is the fact that our kids are experiencing the first African-American President of the United States in Barack Obama—whom I might add was a pretty good basketball player in his earlier days. However, a typical kid from the suburbs of New Jersey like me, with a desire to pursue medicine was few and far between. I remember when *The Cosby Show* debuted in September 1984 and it caused controversy. It was the first of its kind to showcase an African-American family led by a physician and a lawyer. No one on the show went to jail or received public assistance. Although my father was not in the house and was a crack addict, I totally related to *The Cosby Show*. My mother was a successful government official and ultimately finished her career as Assistant Commissioner at the Department of Banking and Insurance for the State of New Jersey. We lived in a middle class neighborhood in South Orange and Princeton. My friends' parents were professionals and all of my aunts and uncles were college graduates. My mother's two brothers, Byron and Donald became a Pharmacist and Emergency Room Physician respectively. At any rate, I knew I had a tough act to follow.

I only had a marginal understanding of race issues prior to transitioning into my new high school curriculum. The first time I was exposed to a racial issue was when my mother and I were driving my sister to her first year of college at Hampton University in Hampton, Virginia. At 12 years old the drive from New Jersey to Virginia may have been the longest ever. I remember how excited I was to put change in the tolls and stop at rest stops for junk food. One particular rest stop would always be remembered. My sister was hungry and I had to go to the bathroom, so mom pulled into a convenience store with a gas station. My sister and I ran into the small store while my mother was at the gas pump. The clerk had his head down when the two of us walked in. My mother soon entered the store ready to pay for her gas. When I came out of the bathroom, I noticed my mom waiting for the teller as if there was a long line and she was at the back of it. Except, there was no one in the store but us.

Mom turned to the clerk and said "I would like ten dollars on pump number five please." Back then $10 filled her tank.

"You are going to have to wait until that woman is done. She was here first," the clerk responded in an annoyed and almost angry tone.

It appeared that he was referring to my sister, but why would mom need to wait for her? My sister approached the counter and the clerk waved my mother and I out of the way so that my sister could bring her Snickers and bag of Funyuns to the counter.

Unsuspecting of the prejudice being shown to my mother, my sister turns toward us and asks "Mom, is it OK if I get these?" The look on the clerk's face was of extreme disbelief. He stuttered, turned a pink shade of red and quickly rang my family up on the register. At first glance my sister does not look like a typical African-American woman. Most people think she is white or Hispanic, but definitely not black. The cashier was biased. He had no idea that we were a family. His racism was challenged that day and I learned a very important lesson. To ensure we understood what had just transpired, my mother explained what racism is and how it has affected African- Americans for hundreds of years. More importantly, she showed me how to not relinquish my power to anyone under any circumstances.

With my new high school transition, it was clear that several teachers, counselors, and administrators may have had preconceived notions about the aptitude of young African-American males and what we could achieve scholastically. My mother and I were successful in ensuring my participation in the more advanced classes. Without having seen my mother tackle these types of obstacles with such quiet grace, I may not have had the wherewithal to battle many of the obstacles I have seen in my life. Witnessing all she had been through while still holding our family together gave me the confidence that I have to this day. I was taught the difference of choosing my battles early on by my mom and a set of unlikely teachers. Thankfully, I learned these lessons well.

A young man must learn that every test, obstacle, situation, battle, adversary or fight can be conquered strategically. Sometimes bowing out of a fight may be best strategy. Too many young men have lost their lives because they were taught to fight a battle without the proper artillery, skill, equipment or capacity to win.

ACTING OUT

I was able to flourish in my new high school environment. It had already been established that I was an intelligent student and my grades reflected as much. I always believed that my grade point average was not the sole indicator of my potential success. I know for a fact that my decision to join other activities also contributed to my success. Through these extracurricular activities, I learned to develop sides of me that I didn't know existed. I joined the drama club and performed in plays and musicals. I played in "Bye Bye Birdie" and smaller stage plays. I also starred as the scarecrow in the musical, "The Wizard of Oz."

My articulation and recitation of a script came with ease. It appeared to me that I was more comfortable in front of a large audience than I was alone with my own thoughts. When I was alone, I thought about my dad a lot. I always asked myself, what can I do for him? Should I do something? Constant thoughts about the well-being of my dad plagued me when I was alone. I heard that he may had fallen on hard times. I wasn't sure and I certainly didn't want to believe it. I hadn't heard from him in over a year to confirm or deny it When I was in public, I was too distracted to think about him which suited me well. On stage, I thought about my next line, my next placement, and presenting a performance that would bring the house down. So many times I wished he were sitting in the theatre watching me perform.

Every time I was on stage I imagined the one empty seat being occupied by him. I found it ironic how I could escape my inner thoughts and realistically become a character, but never escape the longing to have the warm embrace of my dad. After each performance my castmates were greeted by their families. It was if everyone received hugs, accolades and flowers from their fathers. I received those from my family as well, but never from my dad. Above any accolade, or anything else, I yearned for that recognition. Yes, I felt good making my mother and sisters proud, but making my father proud was paramount. There aren't too many things more important to a young man than when his dad smiles and says, "Son, I'm proud of you." I buried those feelings often to great stage success.

It was my high school drama participation that helped prepare me for the public roles which I serve today. In my line of work, I have to stand in front of students and lecture as well as testify in front of jurors. I must deliver the information in a way that can be easily understood while somewhat detaching myself from the loss felt by so many families. As a forensic pathologist, I must be professional at all times and look at a homicide for what it is. Some days I have to examine the dead bodies of young people who appear to be younger versions of myself. Playing a part on stage allowed me to distance myself but be close enough to provide comfort and closure. The part I play now is in the real life horrific drama of so many families who experience sudden and unexpected loss. Today, in my real life drama, there is never a star of the show. I am a leading character who merely becomes a recorder of fact—I am a voice for the voiceless.

MANLY STRATEGY

Varsity football also played a major role in shaping my character and nurturing my ability to lead. Some of my greatest accomplishments in high school were done on the gridiron. I loved the camaraderie of my teammates. The bond between a team is hard to break and I cherished it with pride. Although an average player, I was an above average leader of the young men with whom I shared the field. I was named co-captain of the team because of my ability to lead. I exuded confidence and enthusiasm and I understood what it meant to give and follow directions. Football provided me with something that acting did not—a chance to hone my strategic skills. It is often called a man's game, because it is a very aggressive contact sport—alpha male vs. alpha male. Once again, this was an opportunity for me to prove that the strongest person does not always win a battle. Instead, it is the one who is more strategic. Whenever an opposing player was running full speed directly at me and he outweighed me, I went low on him. I took out his equilibrium and brought him down. In other words, brain over brawn.

Many areas of manhood are equated with sports: strategic game plan, strong work ethic, and a tough mental attitude. Team sports provide young people a context for group success. Being a part of team is a great experience for a boy.

Being a father to young boys now, I see many of the same lessons I learned from coaches as teachable moments for my boys, now seven and eleven—the same age I was when my father was absent from my life. After games, I walk to the car with my arm around my son's shoulder pads to encourage them. I plan to sit in the bleachers on my son's lives like I wanted my dad to sit in on mine.

The true test of anyone seeking to mature is to face
the one obstacle that is seemingly insurmountable.

PHONING HOME

I really thought I was doing OK without my dad. Then he
called one evening. I was expecting that he would call at some point,
and believed I would be prepared when he did. But when I had to
confront my true feelings about my father I failed the test miserably.
It was actually late for someone to be calling. I answered thinking
that it would be a call for my mother. I was right, but had no idea
what the next few seconds would hold.

"Hello."

"Roger, this is your dad." the voice said.

I recall the last words I spoke to my father years ago in Rochester,
"I'm going home and I can't be around you until you get help."
Although I fully expected to speak to him at some point in my life,
I never knew when and I certainly didn't know it would be this
night. Not only was I looking forward to speaking to him, but I
hoped and prayed that he would become active in my life again. At
that moment, the phone was the equivalent of me lining up with
my teammates on the football field and looking into the stands and
being shocked to see my dad there. It was as surprising as looking
into the audience of my school play and seeing him standing in the
back flashing his thousand-watt smile.

The next few moments could have gone a number of ways. I
could have been indifferent. This call could have given me a tremendous amount of joy. Or it could have made me very upset. It had
been years since my dad and I had spoken and not once did he
attempt to reach out to me. Where was he when I needed him?

Where was that arm around my shoulder pads? Why should I care that he left? He obviously doesn't care about me. Why should I care about him?

A man's ability to succeed is not derived in how he sits in times of comfort, but rather how he stands in times of crisis.

In my mind, this was a time of crisis and it overwhelmed me. I started yelling into the phone.

"What do you want? Why are you calling me? After all this time you decided to call me late at night?"

All those years of hurt, neglect and abandonment overpowered me. All those years of bottled up emotions rushed out of my heart, and the words of hurt and humiliation rolled off my tongue. I had lost control and the pain consumed me. Had you asked me if I was OK before this phone call, I would have told you that I was fine. What I failed to realize was that I was bottling up those feelings instead of dealing with them. I had never vented my feeling to anyone.

My mother heard the commotion and came running. She grabbed the phone from me. I'm sure in that moment, she wanted to protect me from the pain and anguish I was experiencing. I know she would have loved to have intercepted that call to spare my feelings. It was too late. I had heard his voice. A voice I hadn't heard in years. Now, for every year I hadn't heard that voice, the brunt of my pain was being unleashed. I stormed away and rushed into my bedroom. In a fit of rage I ripped down my posters of Martin Luther King Jr., Cosmos Soccer, and the Detroit Pistons. Before my mother could console me, I managed to get out of my room and run out the front door. I jumped into the car and slammed the door. With tears in my eyes and thoughts racing a mile a minute, I started the car and sped off to my girlfriend Marcey's house. I knew she would be asleep in her room at this late hour. I screeched to a halt, jumped out of the car, and threw rocks at her window. I screamed her name as loud as I could. Not only did her bedroom light turn on, but so did many other lights in her house and the houses of neighbors who were in earshot. She looked through her window confused. She opened it and asked, "Roger, what in the world is wrong with you?

"You need to come down here now! He called me! He called me!" I screamed through my tears.

"Who called you?"

"My father called me! He called me! Please come down here now! I need you now!"

She closed the window and I walked to the front door and waited for her to come down.

Marcey was the only person I could trust with my emotions.

When I got to the door, Marcey's mother cracked it open. She wasn't inviting me in. Instead, she encouraged me to go home and talk with my mother. She also warned me not to stand under her daughter's window throwing rocks and screaming at the top of my lungs. I knew she was right, but her comment fell on deaf ears since I really needed someone to talk to.

I jumped back into the car and drove to my friend Hugh's house. He was able to calm me down and hear me out. I needed someone to listen and allow me to vent. I needed someone who would not judge my words but recognize my pain. Hugh was my best friend in high school and was there for me. I can never repay him for being there for me that night.

Young men are crying out to have their voices heard. Society teaches men to suck it up and be a man. We are taught from a very young age that it is not manly to cry and vent our feelings. We are told that masculinity is a silent strength. I challenge that notion and many others. Strength is not necessarily reared in silence. A strong man is one who takes care of the things entrusted to him by God.

I raise my sons to know that they need to express themselves. Fortunately, God has always given me a great support system in my mother, my sisters, and a ton of friends. Some of my boys are like brothers to me and they were there for me from the very beginning. I thank God that the voids in my life didn't destroy me. Rather, they were teaching me important lessons and grooming me for my life as an adult and a father. Like any young man, I wanted the approval of my father so bad that I succeeded without realizing it. I worked harder to get something that never came, despite the fact that the grades, the applause and the wins came. I believe that God placed me in this situation to help cultivate my level of maturity. When I look back and see the gaps and voids, it only strengthens my resolve to be a good father to my children. These same voids motivate me to reach back into the community and educate those who are either fathers or in need of a father. It was clear to me then that I had significant healing to do from the absence of my father. Now, at this stage in my life it was time to claim my legacy.

Chapter Five

THE BISON LEGACY

Reared against the eastern sky
Proudly there on hilltop high,
Far above the lake so blue
Stands old Howard firm and true...

- Howard University, Alma Mater

DURING my childhood and high school years I grew into a hard-working young man, both on and off the field. I soon realized how much I savored the feeling of success as a result of my diligence. After studying hard for an exam, I felt a great sense of pride when I passed with a high score. When I worked hard at practice, I became extremely satisfied when my coaches and teammates saw me excel on the field. I knew all of my hard work would once again pay off for the next important chapter of my life—applying to college.

I had my heart set on attending Howard University my entire life. My grandfather was a graduate of Howard and told me countless stories of his time as a student, which made it all the more intriguing for me to attend. I wanted to follow in his footsteps and become a medical doctor. My hard work in my four years of high school prepared me for one day in particular; the day my acceptance letter arrived. I had been checking our mailbox with eager anticipation every day for two weeks. I knew the letter would arrive any day now as other friends had received their letters. What an agonizing feeling when your friends get into their schools of choice and you're still waiting. My heart was set on Howard and the letter could not have come soon enough. The anticipation was unnerving.

The day in April finally arrived. I ran to the mailbox and it was there! I stood in the driveway for a few moments staring and holding the envelope. I left all of the other mail in the box because nothing was more important than this letter. It was a crisp white envelope with a cellophane window. My name and address showed clear through in bold letters. There was royal blue lettering in the top left corner. The university seal was on the envelope and it read "Veritas et Utilitas." Before opening the envelope, I literally closed my eyes and dreamed in black and white. I thought of myself on the campus, making friends and learning. I thought of myself being taught as my grandfather was taught. It was a surreal moment for me as it seemed like time had stopped. If someone told me that I stood there with that envelope for 20 minutes I would have believed it.

I opened my eyes and then opened the envelope. I almost ripped the letter! When I unfolded the letter the first few words dropped me to my knees. **'Congratulations! You have been accepted to Howard University, Class of 1996!'** I cried. This was a monumental moment for me. Tears ran down my face as I thought about the significance of what I was holding in my hands. The legacy that I would now be claiming was extremely important to me and now my journey was beginning. As a young man, I still searched for that sense of belonging to a fatherly family inheritance. Since my father was no longer a part of my life at this point, I identified with my grandfather's journey. My grandfather was well known and respected for helping people. His journey became my journey that I was destined to pursue.

In June 1992 I stepped onto campus for the first time as a student two months before the rest of the freshman class. I entered the pre-matriculation program that Howard offered to pre-med students. The program prepared students for the curriculum that lie ahead. Entering early set a good standard for how I could best equip myself going forward. Howard graduates have made significant impacts on American life in the areas of politics, religion, the arts, media, and of course medicine. I was so fortunate to now be a part of Howard's lineage that the thought overwhelmed me at times. It was clear to me early on as a freshman, that I had to overcome any obstacles before me just like my mother taught me. I was excited that my legacy was beginning at "The Mecca." This was the nickname for the school because its students were at the center of African-American intellectual thought and development.

My Uncle Donald was an ER physician at DC General and he came to pick me up at Union Station. It was my first time on Howard's campus. Uncle Donald dropped me off at Slowe Hall in LeDroit Park off 3rd Street. I did not have a roommate for the 5-week summer program. I remember getting to my room and the AC felt like it was 50 degrees, so I walked into the room of an upperclassman.

"Congratulations! Welcome to The Mecca!"

"Thanks. I'm Roger." He reached out to shake my hand.

"Cool. I'm John." Since this is my last stint here would you like this?

He handed me a Mecca t-shirt. He then gave me a Budweiser store light.

"Thanks!"

"No problem. Good luck!"

The next day I met all of the participants in the pre-matriculation program. I made lots of friends in that program that have remained friends today. I took biology, chemistry and math. I did well because at the end of the program I had the option to actually go into a Bachelors to M.D. Accelerated Program. I made the conscious choice, however, of not going that route. The program leaders were brutally honest regarding the intensity and level of studying required to complete all of your math and sciences in two years as opposed to four. I did not want to miss out on my full college experience as I knew such an intense program would be too much.

A few weeks later I came back as a true freshman. My mother drove me down for my official freshman day. One of the things she told me in the car was "to be careful to measure your expectations of others. No one will work as hard on your behalf as you will for yourself." When mom said things like this I just listened and nodded in agreement. My first roommate, Ray, was a local guy from Maryland. We instantly bonded and he became my roommate all four years. He was a great high school baseball player with an easy-going personality that kept me laughing.

BLEEDING BLUE & WHITE

In the late 80's and early 90's, at the emergence and dawn of Hip-Hop, Howard saw a strong shift toward knowledge of Africa. Students wore African medallions around their necks and dashikis on their backs. Someone spray painted the word AMANDLA over the red, black and green painted continent of Africa on the pavement of the main yard. The emblem of freedom and consciousness remained there for several years until nature washed it away over time. Hip hop groups like Public Enemy had messages of Black pride in their songs and these songs were popular on campus. Being ingrained in the culture at Howard during this time is hard to put into words. We weren't simply dancing to the music; we were internalizing the words. The lyrics had profound meaning and I was never so proud to be a Black man growing up in America than when I was at Howard. My first year experience shaped my future and helped frame the man I am today. Many of the lessons I speak to young men about today and even to my own sons are life lessons I learned at Howard. Those early days at The Mecca were priceless.

It was very common on the campus main yard to hear poets giving oral expression on what it meant to be Black, or hearing gifted musicians from The School of Fine Arts provide an impromptu jam session. Walk a few feet further and you might see a debate between young intellectuals over the African school of thought vs. the African-American way of thinking. The main campus was a training ground of intellectual stimuli, and I loved every minute of it.

The Howard University experience established a vision for the future. We were to be the talented tenth—the leadership for America.

I often walked the halls of the Blackburn Center on campus or Douglass Hall named after the renowned slavery abolitionist Frederick Douglass. I spent time in Founders Library or in Locke Hall named after Alan Locke. I imagined what medical school life must have been like for my grandfather in the 1920's. The fashion was different, but the sense of being at one of the greatest learning institutions for young Black people is the same sentiment that has resonated with each graduating class. When my grandfather attended the Howard University School of Medicine, he met my grandmother who at the time was attending Freedman's Hospital School of Nursing located on the same campus. I'm sure they had a great courtship and discussed their futures together. They may have spoken of getting married and raising a family. Maybe they spoke about where they would choose to live and what type of home they wanted to create for their children.

There comes a time in a man's life where he has conversations of marriage with his future wife and settling down with the woman of his dreams.

Most young men will date plenty of women. Especially on a campus like Howard where there were so many intelligent and beautiful women, so much so that they outnumber the men almost seven to one. It isn't until a man meets the person who he considers "The One" that these types of thoughts begin to surface. I'm sure that's how my grandfather felt when he first began courting my grandmother.

I walked into chemistry class like any other class on any other day. Little did I know that this particular chemistry class would give me a beautiful glimpse of my future. Not that the lesson was overwhelming or the professor's lecture life-changing. None of those reasons made this day so special. It was her. I had seen Angelique Hendricks a Microbiology major before. When I saw her this time in the auditorium, I almost lost my breath because of her fly Halle Berry haircut. We even knew some of the same people. But this time I had something to prove. She was one of the most beautiful women I had ever met. She had a style about her that I had rarely seen. As a matter of fact, she had a unique DC swagger that I only noticed about women from the immediate area. Being a Jersey boy myself, this intrigued me and I had to get to know her. I knew that we already had a love for science in common. At first, she was not too interested in me. One day, I was up around 6:30 AM on a Saturday morning and on my way to the microbiology laboratory for a study group. As I did every Saturday, I stopped by the Cafeteria to get a quick bowl of Cap'N Crunch. It was my favorite. She was there. When I saw her in the cafeteria that day I knew this was my opportunity to introduce myself again. Knowing that the falling pencil would never get her attention, I said "hello" and told her I would love to get to know her. I gave her my phone number and hoped she called. Two weeks later, she did. What took her so long?

After sharing our love of poetry and a few more conversations, I soon realized that she too was raised by a single mother. Angelique understood me. She related to the stories I had to tell. Not only could she listen and smile, but she could share and cry. I felt comfortable around her. I felt a safety that I had never experienced with a woman before.

I had great friendships with both men and women at Howard. None gave me the sense of belonging that I had with Angelique. I felt like our lives mirrored each other's as we had so much in common. As I only have sisters, Angelique has a twin sister, Nikki who also attended Howard University. She also had an older sister, older brother, and a younger brother. Most in common was that Angelique shared a burning desire to have a relationship with her father. Angie's father died when she was young and like me, that loss left a void in her life. She never experienced dancing with her father at daddy daughter dances. I had no memories of my dad coming to my games. She had no memories of celebrating her daddy on Father's Day. Neither did I. It became apparent to me that we had a bond and that it was a special one. Angelique and I dated for most of our time at Howard. I knew I wanted to spend the rest of my life with her and I eventually asked her to do just that after I graduated. It's amazing how closely my journey through young adulthood mimicked that of my grandfather as opposed to my father. I embraced the journey that was given to me.

The confidence and pride that came with being a student at Howard is still hard to describe. There was a sense of safety that enveloped us as students. This safety was not a false sense of security, but a real understanding that what we were learning would prepare us to become leaders in America. I was at a monumental point in my life and I had to keep my focus if I was going to be successful. It became increasingly important for me to realize my dreams. Not to prove anything to anyone else, but to prove it to myself. During my time at Howard I understood that hard work was the great equalizer. I was never the smartest in the classroom, or the most talented on stage, and those that know me knew that I was not the fastest or the biggest on the football field. But I worked hard and was dedicated.

Like my grandfather, I had successfully matriculated through Howard. I had an example of manhood. As a matter of fact, I encountered many examples of manhood. All of the men I met during my tenure have remained close to me today. We worked hard and we played hard. I will never forget the party house at 748 Rock Creek Church Road. Throughout our time at Howard we challenged each other to be and do better. When we needed to study we reminded each other of upcoming tests. When we were studying too hard, we reminded each other to take a break. We built accountability for each other. It's funny, the world may suggest that men of color who are accountable, capable, dedicated, and disciplined are a rarity. Anyone who believes that has never stepped on the yard at Howard University, nor have they read the alumni roster.

I had studied and achieved academic success. I had risen to leadership positions within the organizations I chose to serve. I had fun and partied. I attended the football and basketball games. I wore the coveted Campus Pal T-shirt with my name on the back. I met the love of my life and asked her to be my wife. Most of all, I followed a legacy deeply rooted in the fabric of this country, a legacy not lost nor stolen. A legacy of free men no longer slaves. I am a free man who is now charged and ready to free others.

Chapter Six

LEADING THE PACK

"If your actions inspire others to dream more,
learn more, do more, and become more,
you are a leader."

- John Quincy Adams

I never shied away from being a leader. When I was in middle school I was a member of student council and the 6th grade President. I remember I had to make a poster for school the next day to tell everyone what office we were running for. I was running for Treasurer because I wanted to be in charge of the money. My mother's friend Greg heard about me running and wanted to see the poster.

"Why are you running for Treasurer?"

"Because the Treasurer deals with the money!"

"Is it too late to run for President?"

"No. I just have to make a new poster for President."

"Well, I think you should make your sign and run for President. As President you not only control the money, but you control where the money goes."

"Oh. I never thought about that. Thanks."

Not only did I become 6th grade President, I became 7th grade President and in 8th grade I became School President. I enacted policies to bring more snacks in the school store like Doritos and

Now and Later's. We improved the school dance by promoting tuxedos and limos.

Leadership is not about being someone who others follow, but about how that leader is willing to serve those around him.

Leading in middle school and high school was great preparation for Howard. I was anxious to lead. I was introduced to a group of students called the Campus Pals whose purpose is to help new students with the demands of matriculating as freshman. What began as a classroom project, the Campus Pals continue to provide support for young people entering into the university. What impressed me about this group of students was their enthusiasm. They were always happy, laughing and eager to help every single day. If you had a question about where to go, a Campus Pal would not only inform you, but they'd probably walk you there. It was easy to get to know them because they wore shirts with their names on the back. For the first few weeks of school, they had activities for the freshman and put on a variety show, a dating game, a trip to Kings Dominion, and an ice cream networking social. The Pals were the epitome of what I saw in myself; a very willing spirit to help and serve others.

I knew I wanted to be in a service organization that helped mentor young people. I was a mentor in high school and mentoring was a reflection of the presence of great men, women and peers in my life. This was the same reason I chose to major in Biology. I wanted to help people. I knew what it was like to be helpless, alone and abandoned. When I found out that the Pals were holding auditions for interested students, I attended and expressed an interest in becoming a part of this group my sophomore year. I went through the audition process and was selected.

Becoming a member of the Camps Pal's was a true blessing. From the outside looking in, the organization looked like a bunch of students committed to helping freshman and having a lot of fun in the process. From the inside, I saw the logistical planning it took to arrange a variety show in a large theater. I witnessed the student leaders of the group organize charter buses to transport every Howard freshman to Kings Dominion two hours away. Not only did we take the entire class, but we provided them with lunch at the park. This took an extreme amount of logistical planning and as an insider I got to see the wheels in motion. This was just the type of experience I needed as I was on my way to becoming a young man of purpose.

I have always been the kind of person to lead and make my own way. I never had a pity party for the things I didn't have. Instead, I championed the things I had and used them to propel myself. This trait was personified at Howard. By senior year I became the president of the Campus Pal organization. I became so interested in taking on leadership positions and was also fortunate enough to serve as campaign manager and then Chief of Staff to a successful presidential run for the Howard University Student Association (HUSA). I ran the day-to-day activities of the student government, which provided additional training in leadership. These experiences continued to build upon the legacy that already served as the foundation for my future successes.

Chapter Seven

CRACKED MANHOOD

"When wealth is lost, nothing is lost,
when health is lost, something is lost,
when character is lost, all is lost."

-Billy Graham

ONCE I became adjusted to college, my life felt *almost* complete. I had the grades, a great girl, and plenty of friends. I had my desired social status and belonged to great organizations. I was becoming a success in my own right. What I lacked was a dad to share it with. I was in high school the last time I heard my father's voice, and it threw me for a serious loop. I wasn't expecting his call that evening and certainly was not as prepared for it as I had hoped. At this point in my life, however, I felt a little more equipped to speak with him. It's one thing if he called me unexpectedly, but I was in control if I reached out to him.

As time went on, a burning desire to find and speak to my dad continued to grow. I didn't have anything in particular to say to him, but I never let go of the notion that he should be a meaningful part of my life. He was missing out on key events and I may have been missing out on his. I made my first attempt to find my father since that 4th of July weekend when I visited him in Rochester as a child. I called my mother to see if she had any information as to his whereabouts. Surprisingly, she gave me everything I needed. My mother is my angel. She could have given me his information a long time ago, but she wanted to wait until I asked. I guess she knew I would have inquired eventually. Had she given me the information to find my father any sooner, it may have been devastating for me. She felt that I was mature enough to handle it and I also felt I was ready. I was on a mission to find him like when I made up my mind at 10 years old to take a cab to his job. Little did I know, however, that there was another heavy blow waiting for me.

I found out that my father wasn't doing well. I tracked him down in a homeless shelter in Atlantic City. I took time away from school to make this trip. When I got there I immediately found his bunk based on how neat his personal belongings were and how the blankets were folded on the cot. My dad was a military man and was always sharp in his appearance. That bunk definitely gave him away. Dad wasn't there but I was told he was dating a woman across town and I was given her address.

When I arrived at this woman's place, I hesitated before I knocked on the door. I wasn't sure what I was going to find once it opened. Would I see my father? Would I see his new wife? Would I meet another family? Would I meet another son? I braced myself for whatever was about to happen. I knocked hard and after a slight moment of silence, the door opened and there stood my father. The man whose voice I hadn't heard since the day he called the house and threw me into a rage.

My father greeted me first with a smile. Surprisingly, it was the same smile I remember as a child. He seemed genuinely happy to see me as he looked me up and down. The last time he saw me in person, I was a lot shorter with no facial hair. Before him stood a grown man—still lacking facial hair. A man that he fathered but did not raise to become a man. My father stood back for a few more seconds and took in the idea of looking at his son in the face, for the first time in a very long time.

I shook my dad's hand and greeted him. It was an awkward moment to say the least as neither of us knew whether we should hug, shake hands, break down and cry, or simply catch up. I took the safe road and shook his hand. He invited me in and closed the door behind me. We sat down at the woman's kitchen table. The awkward small talk began as we caught one another up on each other's our lives. Then a very odd thing happened. As terribly ill-suited as it was, my father decided to take this opportunity to pass some "wisdom" along to me. Every first time father dreams of the day that he can teach his son to play catch, tie his shoes, or tie a necktie. Good dads teach their sons. When a son has a question about girls, a good dad looks forward to having that conversation. He may not know exactly what to say, but he definitely wants to impart some lesson on his son.

The pride in a man is immense when his son is coming up in his footsteps.

The other side of the coin is that there are bad fathers who still want to teach their sons. In this surreal moment, I sat at the kitchen table of a woman whom I did not know. I sat with a man who was homeless and shared the same first and last name that was no longer recognizable. Now dad had an overwhelming desire to teach me something important.

Higher baby
Get higher baby!
Get higher baby!
And don't ever come down!
Freebase!

- *"White Lines," Grand Master Flash & The Furious Five*

My father began to describe and demonstrate how to prepare cocaine for free-basing. I was shocked but my body froze and I could not move. I sat quietly as he kept talking as if he were making me a can of Ravioli like when I was a child. He explained how the water is prepared and when to add baking soda. He described the recipe to the exact detail, including what the flame setting should be on a gas stove and how it is better than the electric stove. I thought he was going to cook it and smoke it right in front of me. My vision was blurred as I could not believe that this was my father. Instantly I did not hate him. I felt deeply sorry for him. I longed even more to help him. He was a thousand miles away from the man that I used to know and admire.

Dad finished the conversation as if we had been talking with each other all along. Luckily, I wasn't expecting an apology or an explanation, because I would have been highly disappointed. I simply wanted to see him. I needed some type of closure to determine if we could ever have a meaningful relationship.

A million magic crystals, painted pure and white
A multi-million dollars almost overnight
Twice as sweet as sugar, twice as bitter as salt
And if you get hooked baby, it's nobody else's fault,
So don't do it!
*"White Lines," Grand Master
Flash & the Furious Five*

When I left the woman's house, I seriously pondered what I had just witnessed. So many emotions ran through me at the same time. My father was homeless and addicted to crack. The ride back to DC was a lot longer that night. I left my father's world and returned to my world, a legacy, my destiny at Howard. So now, with my father clearly unable to fill the void that his absence had left, I had to start the healing process. Although, I was not yet ready to forgive him, I was indeed ready move on.

Chapter Eight

MOUNTAIN TO A MOLE HILL

"You may not control all of the events that happen to you,
but you can decide not to be reduced by them."

- Dr. Maya Angelou

WHEN I entered Howard University, I knew I wanted to be a physician and scientist. From the time I was two and a half I sat on my dad's lap watching *Quincy* and wore my Fisher Price Doctor Kit around the house. I dreamt of being a doctor and was eager to help and treat people. One of the first scientific classes I took at Howard University was biology. The science and medical majors at Howard take classes in an area on campus called "The Valley;" four buildings on a lower incline than the main campus. In The Valley, there is the Physics Department, the Chemistry Department, the Biology Department, and the School of Pharmacy. I felt an air of intimidation and respect as these historic buildings housed some of the greatest scientific minds to grace the African-American race and our world.

When I entered the Biology Department at Just Hall, I was a young man looking to do great things with my life and eager to learn the steps needed to do so. I walked into class ready to soak up all the knowledge a professor could throw at me. I was so anxious to fulfill a legacy. I had to succeed and knew what success looked like and was ready to make it happen...or so I thought. I took my first biology exam and failed it! Up until that point I had never failed a test—ever!

It is important for young people to dream and consider personal goals for their future. With all the distractions from today's society, more emphasis needs to be placed upon the dreams of young people. It is clear that a child's dream can come true. I dreamed it, pursued it, and achieved it.

As prepared as I was for college, the one thing I wasn't prepared for was a failing grade. I wasn't quite sure what to do. I went through each question over and over in my mind. I was sure that I knew the answers and I began to question my own intelligence. Did I really know? Maybe I didn't study long or hard enough. Maybe I should schedule a meeting with the biology professor. Should I call mom? With all of these unanswered questions, there was one question that I did have the answer to. That question was "How are you going to bounce back Roger?" I immediately felt the same energy and confidence I had fending for myself in Rochester when my dad abandoned me. I had to put the first exam behind me and prepare for the second one, even though I had so many unanswered questions. I knew I had to move on. Besides, I told myself, it's not the end of the world; is not like a midterm or final. I studied longer and more diligently. When I took the second exam, I had a new focus and a new spirit. I was definitely ready. I arrived on the morning of the test anxious, but confident. I could not believe I took my second biology exam and failed it!

The questions that were surfacing were now frightening. Failing the first time could be explained away. It was my first college biology exam, I was anxious and nervous and just wasn't quite prepared.

Failing the second exam forced me to question if I deserved to be there. I had been headed in the direction of a medical career my entire life. It was the profession I strongly desired and never even considered another career goal. Maybe now that it was time for me to "put up," I just couldn't cut it. I watched the reactions of other students when they received their exams back. Some received a grade of 100%. Others received 95%. Still, others received 90%. What did they know that I didn't? After failing the first exam, I would have settled for a 70% which some students got. I however, failed with a 62%. It felt weird hearing students complain about a grade of 75% when at this point, I would have been happy to get a 75%. I felt like a failure and that my hopes and dreams would not come to pass.

I didn't know what else to do. I spoke to one of my close friend's Umar about my two failed exams and how I was feeling. His advice and encouragement were just the words I needed to hear. I had previously shared my background with him so he was familiar with the various trials I faced prior to attending Howard. What he shared has stuck with me for the rest of my life. His words were simple, yet profound and I have often referred back to them in encouraging others.

Umar asked me, "What mountains have you had to climb in your past?"

"How many obstacles have you faced?" "Where these mountains worth climbing?"

"If you knew the day would come that you would sit at the base of this newest obstacle, crying about how hard it was to overcome, would you have climbed all the others before this one?"

How could I sit at this new mountain crying about how steep it was when I had overcome so many mountains already? How dare I worry about my feet being unsteady while climbing this new mountain?

Umar pointed out that if I did that, then every mountain I had climbed and overcome to this point meant nothing!

His words were both hurtful and helpful at the same time. They made me reflect on a childhood which sometimes had uncertainty. I was forced to remember all of my dad's broken promises and my disappointments in him when I was eight years old. What was the point of overcoming what I had been through if I was going to stop now? Why get so close and quit? Even though his words were cutting, I knew that he was absolutely right

A good father speaks life into his children. This is a spiritual and natural requirement in building a strong family. Words can come from anyone but the words of a father have special meaning and takes on life.

Since I couldn't call my father, I called my mom. In so many of my mountaintop experiences in my past, mom was the rock I needed. Mom provided the nurturing of a mother and the strength of a father at the same time.

If you are blessed enough to have people around you, encouraging and telling you the truth about yourself, then success can come that much easier. Everyone needs someone to help us make the right choices toward success, whether it be peers, parents, or other adults that love and admonish you to reach your true potential.

Once I had been reassured by my friend Umar and now my mom, I took on different study habits. I identified a core study group and worked with them daily. My entire study group wanted to be successful doctors also. We made sure we helped each other.

Focused participation in a study group and new study habits placed me in a position to do better in class and on exams. I learned that balance was the most important ingredient towards my personal success; I needed to balance my job at the local sports apparel store, my studies, and my social life. When I understood my process, success followed. I got a 75% on the next examination, and by the end of the semester I had all A's and B's. I never again took my time at Howard for granted. This was a lesson that has stayed with me through life. I don't ever take my walk with God, my family, my friends, or my community for granted.

Chapter Nine

PREPARING FOR THE DRAFT

"The price of success is hard work, dedication to the job
at hand, and the determination that whether we win or lose,
we have applied the best of ourselves to the task at hand."

Vince Lombardi

IT felt good to have the general studying and time management
process under control. The stage was set for the pursuit of my
dream to become a doctor. The first thing I considered was seeking
a job that coincided with my studies to prepare me for my life in
medicine. There are thousands of aspects to the study of medicine so
the opportunities were endless for career development. It was made
clear to me early on by professors and college advisors that in order
to get accepted into medical school I needed to pursue opportunities
in the medical or research settings sooner than later.

I was dating Angie at the time and it was the summer between
my freshman and sophomore year at Howard. I wanted to work in
DC so that I could be close to her. I did not have a job lined up
but told my mother otherwise. Sorry mom. Early in the summer I
finally got a job as women's shoe salesman at JC Penny during the
day and worked as a clerk at Walden Books in the evening. I was a
pretty good sales person—definitely a chip off the old block. I often
thought, a 19 year old young man selling shoes to women wasn't a
bad gig at all. I had a strong work ethic and top sales to show for
it. One of my co-workers, an older black man, witnessed my work

ethic. I shared my dreams of one day becoming a doctor. I could not believe it when he told me that he was an EKG technician at a local hospital. He offered to introduce me to his supervisor Ms. McQueen. Upon meeting Ms. McQueen, it was clear that she saw me like she saw her own children. She too was impressed by my goals and wanted to help me. Thank you Ms. McQueen for giving me a chance.

I became an EKG technician at a local hospital in DC the fall of 1993. An EKG is a test that records the electrical rhythm produced by and controls the heart. I was responsible for performing portable EKG tests at a patient's bedside. The test results were printed and provided to the attending physician and sometimes a cardiologist for interpretation. One of my biggest regrets is that I did not take the opportunity to become proficient in the EKG interpretation by asking more questions.

I will never forget a patient that solidified my interest in medicine. It was a very rainy day in Washington DC. I remember not being able to ride my bike to work that day because of the weather. I was in the Cardiology Unit in the hospital when I got paged to the Trauma Unit. It was not common for portable EKG to be paged to the Trauma bay. Upon my arrival, I was asked to wait because the patient was being air-lifted to the hospital. I was so excited! At this point, I had served as an EKG tech for over a year and was well known by the hospital staff. A young lady arrived as the trauma patient. The environment was hectic but everyone knew what they were doing. She was on a rigid back board, unconscious with a cervical spine collar around her neck and a tube in her throat. Her head was bloody and she appeared dead. The nurses and doctors were working diligently to save her life.

The portable EKG would not be needed, but the attending physician who I had met in the cafeteria several months earlier, turned to me and said "I don't know why they called an EKG Technician for this patient but Roger I know you want to be a doctor so you should stay and watch this!" Nervous and excited, I nodded. The doctors said she had a head injury. They made a small incision in her scalp and inserted a drill. The drill was the manual hand-held type with a crank. The doctor made a whole in her skull to release the pressure on the brain caused by the bleeding in her head. This was called a Burr Hole, which I learned about in biology class. Honestly, I was a bit nauseous when I saw the woman's head jerk back as the drill was inserted. The last thing I wanted to be known for was the EKG Tech who collapsed in the middle of the floor while a procedure was going on. I never became nauseous during a medical or surgical procedure again, and I saw many since my days as an EKG Technician. The physicians and medical staff saved a woman's life that day. It was amazing! There was absolutely no doubt in my mind that wanted to be a doctor. This was important hands-on work that benefitted me greatly.

Young people should apply for internships and jobs to get actual training and experience in the career they desire to work in. Experience is life's best teacher.

At the end of my junior year, I still worked at the hospital, but now in the Medical Supply Department, while still working at a clothing store in Georgetown. During the summer between my junior and senior year I identified a research position at the Howard University Center for Sickle Cell Disease with a PhD researcher. My job required preparing DNA samples to be studied in a search for immunity within HIV infected cells. The research position was an unpaid internship, although I received a small stipend from the University. It seemed like I worked every waking hour during those days; once I left my job at the hospital as an EKG Technician, I headed to the Sickle Center, after which, I went to my job selling clothes in Georgetown. Hardwork and dedication pays off!

THE TRIAL OF THE CENTURY

People of the State of California vs. Orenthal James Simpson

"If it doesn't fit, you must acquit."

- Johnnie Cochran

When I was working at the Sickle Center, the infamous OJ Simpson trial took center stage on TV sets across the nation. CourtTV aired the trial and it was unlike anything the world had ever seen. Simpson was accused of a horrific double homicide of his ex-wife Nicole Brown and her friend Ronald Goldman. More than 200,000 news outlets covered the case that lasted nearly nine months. A key area of importance in the trial was the forensic evidence and how it was handled. Who can forget the late attorney Johnnie Cochran's closing message to the jury, "If it doesn't fit, you must acquit!" There was a set of bloody gloves, blood spatter in a truck, a great deal of evidence at the crime scene, as well as witness testimony of tampering with evidence. The O.J. trial had it all! Like most Americans, I was glued to the TV. There were reports that stated during the trial that the loss of productivity from employees watching the O.J. trial instead of working was estimated at $40 billion. The perspective on the forensic science in this trial caused me to look at my desired profession in an entirely new light. My eyes were immediately opened to the need for science in law. Never before had I considered such a perspective, but this trial and my current work at the Sickle Center sealed it for me. I realized that I wanted to be a forensic scientist!

I turned my attention to learning all that I could about a career as a forensic scientist. The more I learned through my research, the stronger the desire came for me to live this dream. I had already taken the Medical College Admissions Test (MCAT), but this was something new. I was not afraid to change direction and pursue the unknown. What did I have to lose? I was at the bottom of another mountain and instead of contemplating the height, I spit on each hand rubbed them together and began to climb. I specifically wanted to be a forensic biologist; a DNA scientist. Just before my graduation from Howard, I applied to several laboratories on the east coast. Most of the labs required their scientist to be law enforcement agents. However, there was one organization looking to move law enforcement special agents out of the laboratories and replace them with civilian scientists. This was exactly what I was looking for! This well-known organization was the Federal Bureau of Investigations, or commonly referred to as, the FBI.

I cannot say that a career with the FBI was a dream come true because as a child and a teenager, I never dreamed of working for them. Like most people, I had heard of the FBI and could easily assume by their name what their responsibilities were but I didn't really know. The FBI has a secret and mysterious aura about them. As a young person, when I thought of the FBI, I thought of men in dark suits and dark hats. I thought everything was a secret and they passed notes to one another instead of speaking in person. Working for the FBI was another opportunity to succeed. It was the culmination of years of hard work and executed discipline. Working hard in high school afforded me to go to Howard. Now working hard at Howard afforded me a job with the FBI. All the mountain climbing experiences, coupled with the low valley moments culminated into applying for this position. Some may have thought that I was not fully qualified for the position, but what I do know is that God qualifies who He calls.

When I received the call for an interview, I have to admit that I wasn't surprised. It was like I was being drafted into the "Pro's." College was about to be over and now it was time to go into the "league." Like anyone, I prepared hours and hours for this opportunity. I wanted to be picked. I wanted to play at the highest level. There was no higher level than the FBI. What I didn't know but would later learn was that there were approximately 2,000 applications submitted to the FBI for three open positions. An estimated 250 were actually read, and 50 people were granted interviews.

The interview process was what you would have expected. I met with a group of men in dark suits. They asked me of my vision for a future with the Bureau. They asked me who I was and what I wanted to be. The most difficult portion of the process was the "lie detector test." I will never forget being asked the most generic questions. It seemed pretty easy at first. What I could not explain was that with the history of drug addiction in my family, even the easiest questions surrounding drug abuse caused me a huge amount of anxiety. I was attached to wires on the tips of my fingers with a cord around my chest, and a blood pressure cuff on my right arm. Talk about nervous. All I kept thinking about was my father. Two weeks later I found out that I failed the lie detector test. However, I got a call from Special Agent Jack Quill who told me that I would get another chance. He said, "Mitchell, you need to pass it this time, we don't take liars in the Bureau". I responded "Yes Sir". Given another chance I passed. Six months prior to my graduation from Howard University, I received the phone call I had been waiting for. I was one of the three. I had been hired by the FBI as a forensic biologist! Look at God!

All I had to do now was graduate!

Nothing is easy. Never forget that. From kick-off to the end of the game, never give up!

Chapter Ten

FROM BOYS TO MEN

"I've discovered new parts of my manhood,
places I couldn't get to without loving someone
else unconditionally and putting others before myself."

- Derek Fisher

FOR some strange reason, deep inside I felt that my freedom would not commence until I graduated from Howard. May 11, 1996, was graduation day. I was ecstatic to be a college graduate, and more specifically, a Howard University graduate. I did it in four years-with honors!

Graduation from a college or university is a special occasion. Students successfully matriculate through a college experience and have achieved academic success as well as gained life lessons, social awareness, and transitioned into adulthood. Anything worth achieving is a process. Staying true to the process is really where your success lies.

I was so excited that Pop Thompson and his family agreed to attend my graduation along with my mother, sisters and a host of other family members. Now that I was fulfilling one part of my career goal, I thought back to that day when I held the acceptance letter from Howard in my hand. When it came, I wept. I was overwhelmed at the thought of following in my grandfather's footsteps. I realized that the blessing of attending Howard had skipped a generation and landed on me, and for that, I was so grateful. My anticipation had now moved from wanting to hold an acceptance letter in my hand to wanting to hold a degree. I was only days away from obtaining my degree, wishing farewell to my college which would now be my alma mater, and moving on to the next phase of my life. I was in my dorm room when I received the phone call that instantly challenged my thinking.

"Hello."

"Roger this is mom. How you doin'?"

"I'm fine mom. How are you? Things OK?"

"I'm fine. I need to let you know that your father is coming to your graduation."

There was a moment of silence. I needed several moments, to process what my mother had said. What? Why now? This is by far the biggest day of my life! I had never imagined that in the next 24 hours I would look out towards the bleachers and see my father. This was something that I had wanted since childhood. Now that it was here, I didn't know if I still wanted it. My mind raced with thoughts as to whether I would be OK with my absentee father overshadowing my accomplishments on my big day. This was the ultimate irony. Did I want my father to participate in my success after all of these years? Yes. Did I want answers to my questions? Yes. Did I want Mr. Thompson, who has been more of a dad to me than my own father to feel slighted by my dad's attendance? Did I want to break down crying at my Howard University commencement? No!

"OK mom. If he wants to come I am fine with it."

"That's great Roger, I'll let him know."

When the day arrived, I lined up with thousands of graduating classmates. There were lots of smiles, hugs, photos, flowers, cards, and gifts. Family members spilled out from everywhere. Excitement filled the air for as far as I could see. I tried my best to contain my anxiousness behind my smile. Behind my smile was the nervous feeling of the unknown. In a matter of minutes, I would see Roger Mitchell Sr, the man who is responsible for my birth; the same man who responsible for my pain. The man I hadn't seen for half of my life.

The graduation ceremony began and all of the graduates walked from the campus theater to the main campus for the commencement speech. Everyone was waving, screaming, holding up banners, and clapping. As loud as was, I tuned it all out. Instead, I'm doing the one thing I've been doing since I was 10 years old; searching the bleachers for my father. Face after face….that's not him…another face…that is not him. Maybe if I found my mother in the crowd…. No that's not him. I have to admit that I don't remember the commencement speech. I imagine that the speech was the typical words of encouragement to be leaders and to not take anything for granted. My future was at hand. After the speech was over and every name called, I turned to locate my family and celebrate this victory.

When I noticed my family, it brought me nothing but smiles. I saw the Thompson family and I saw my mom. Hugh was there too. Next to my mother, I saw my dad. I walked directly up to Mr. Thompson and he opened his arms to embrace me. Mr. Thompson is a tall man who can envelope you in a bear hug. That's exactly what I wanted and it's exactly what he did. His hug to me meant, "Roger, I'm so proud of you. The odds were stacked against you. There were times you were uncertain. There were times you may have wanted to give up but you never did! Today is your day! Today is the end of one life and the beginning of another. I am so proud of you." In turn, my hug to Mr. Thompson was a way of saying "Thank you Mr. Thompson. You have been the father that I lacked in my life. You embraced me like I was one of your sons and I am forever grateful. I hope I have made you proud of me as I now stand as a college graduate."

I took a step back from Pop Thompson and looked to my left. I saw my mother and father looking at me and smiling. I approached my mother. When I looked in her face, I saw behind her smile. She was more concerned for me than I was for myself. Her eyes asked, "Are you OK?" My smile reassured her that I was fine. I hugged my mother. She embraced me and told me that she loved me. I then turned to my dad.

"You look skinny." I smiled and extended my hand toward him to shake his hand.

He took my hand and smiled. "You look good Roger. I'm proud of you son."

I promised my family that I would see them shortly at my sister's house in Maryland for the graduation barbeque. I turned and rejoined the procession of graduates off the yard. The band continued play. The festivities continued. None of that mattered to me anymore. I had just shaken hands with my father who hadn't been a part of my life for many years. More importantly, I harbored no hard feelings or ill will. I accepted his words of congratulations. I now felt the true transition from boyhood to manhood. I had faced the one thing in my life that was the most troubling. This time I passed the test. The last time I heard my father's voice, he was teaching how to free-base cocaine. As a fifteen year old boy I had thrown a tantrum when I heard his voice over the phone. As a man, I could face the fact that he hasn't been there and didn't do what he was supposed to do as a father. I can face the fact that he left me and my family. I faced these issues because men realize that there are lessons in all things. Instead of harboring bitterness and contempt, as a man, I choose to use what he did as an example of what I won't do.

> "Keep on learning, keep on growing,
> Cause wisdom helps us understand
> We're maturing, without knowing,
> These are the things that change boys to men…"
>   - *"Boys to Men," New Edition*

I thank God for the strength to take this lesson and use it for my good, the good of my family, and the good of my work in communities as a mentor and voice for the voiceless. I thank God because ultimately this lesson has transformed me from a boy to a man. When I entered Howard University, I was a boy pursuing a dream and following in the footsteps of my grandfather. When I left Howard University, I was a forensic biologist working for the FBI.

Chapter Eleven

THE QUINCY IN "ME"

"When you catch a glimpse of your potential
that's when passion is born."

- Zig Ziglar

MY life was so much better after having attended Howard. I was now a 22-year- old Black man starting at the FBI in January of 1997. This was before today's TV shows like *CSI, NCIS,* or *Law and Order* graced our homes and made forensic science a cool form of entertainment. In my case this was not entertainment—it was real life. My tenure at the FBI began as a serologist. My job was to identify biological fluids on items of evidence from violent crimes. From sexual assaults, bank robberies, to homicides and home invasions. I served as a case manager ensuring the items of evidence was triaged to the proper area of the laboratory. I had the pleasure of learning from several great forensic scientists at the FBI and was also grateful for the opportunity to serve as the Serology Team Leader for the Unit. Our lab was very busy. Imagine examining the clothing of a seven-year-old girl looking for blood and semen on her small underclothes, socks, and her Strawberry Shortcake T-shirt and shorts. Examining these types of cases was my first exposure to how pervasive violence is in our communities. Victim after victim, young and old, injured and wounded at the hands of another human being.

There were so many cases, but one that I will never forget was when I received a floral dress, pantyhose, and undergarments from a woman who was sexually assaulted at work. I could still smell her perfume coming off of her clothing. The victim reported being at the ATM machine when a man walked up behind her and said, "Are you getting enough money out for me?" Startled, the female victim replied "Oh....no, I barely have enough for myself." She did not think much of this man and returned back to her office. Twenty minutes later, she was on the phone and the man approached her from behind and placed duct tape around her eyes. With a whisper he said, "If you scream, I will kill you and your children!" He sexually assaulted her, robbed her and put duct tape on her mouth, hands, and feet, and left her helpless on her office floor. My first thought was, she had no idea that she would be sexually assaulted that day when she woke up and got dressed. Story after story, people were suffering. People were being injured and killed. I read and processed case-after-case. I was serving my country by helping solve these cases.

Soon after I was hired by the FBI I was chosen as an Employee Assistance Program (EAP) coordinator for the DNA Unit. One of my roles was to be responsive to scientists and agents who were exposed to violence in a way that may affect their ability to work or live. This type of exposure may have come in the form of firing a weapon in the line of duty to the chronic exposure to the examination of forensic evidence. As a function of my new role, I received training in Critical Incident Stress Management as well as Post Traumatic Stress Disorder (PTSD) or "Shell-Shock".

This training gave me the context to understand the violence displayed in my FBI case work. I soon became aware of the cycle of violence. It became clear to me that exposure to violence could create an environment within individuals where they may be more prone to resolve their own conflicts through violence. Violent situations beget violent responses. This work became intriguing for me and for nine months I studied and researched the literature. The research indicated that individuals who had been exposed to violence had a higher anxiety and increased propensity toward a violent reaction.

Exposure to violence may lead to violence. This is part of the stress reaction seen in the PTSD found in communities suffering from chronic violence.

It wasn't until I met the local medical examiner that it all came together for me like a puzzle. All of the forensic biologist's at the FBI had an opportunity to visit the Office of the Chief Medical Examiner in Washington DC. For most of us, this was our first exposure to the forensic pathologist. Each time a doctor walked in dressed in a long white coat, he spoke with authority as he described the autopsy examination procedure. We all listened attentively as we stood in a cold room with steel tables, wooden cutting boards, and steel scalpel handles with long sharp blades. The doctor spoke of his findings seen in homicides and suicides, and the most common causes of death. I raised my hand and asked,

"Are you a PhD or a medical doctor?"

"I'm an MD, I went to medical school."

I was amazed! This man was a forensic pathologist and a physician. When I thought of everything I had done up until that point, my love for science and biology, my passion for disciplined research, my new interest in forensic science and experience at the FBI, my future path became crystal clear. At this point, I knew exactly what type of physician I wanted to be and I became excited about it. I wanted to be a Forensic Pathologist and study violence. As a medical examiner, I would be in a much better position to articulate the end result of violence. Upon realizing this and accepting it as my destiny, I applied to medical school in late 1997.

"If not before me, by me."

- Dr. Roger Mitchell, Jr.

Chapter Twelve

A SON'S FORGIVENESS

For if you forgive other people when they sin against you, your heavenly Father will also forgive you. But if you do not forgive others their sins, your Father will not forgive your sins.

-Matt. 6:14-15

I was eager to start the medical school application process. Anyone applying to graduate school understands that there are tens of thousands of deserving students vying for a few open positions in the top schools. Similar to the process that I went through in applying for the open position at the FBI, medical school is also a selective process where only the best are given the nod of acceptance.

In the midst of me feeling the most confident that I had ever been, I received a phone call that would shake my confidence to its very core. I wasn't prepared for my father's call like when I was a teenager. This one rendered me speechless. It was a Saturday evening and I was in my apartment in Hyattsville, Maryland. My home phone rang.

"Hello."

"Roger... Roger is that you?"

The man's voice was deep and familiar. I recognized it... but it had been a couple of years. I hadn't spoken to him since my graduation from Howard.

"Dad?"

"Yes son. It's me. I don't have much time... I'm on a pay phone!

But I need you to come get me" he said. I had waited a long time to hear those words. Now that I am hearing it, it caught me off guard and I was not prepared. On the other end of the line is the man who gave me life. The irony of this situation is that the four words I needed to say to him, he is now saying to me, "I need you Roger."

Oh my God!

"Dad... where are you? Where are you calling me from? Are you okay?

"I'm in Atlantic City. I hit rock bottom but I need to get my life together. This time is gonna be different son. I need help. Can you... can you come get me?"

I immediately thought back to myself at eight years old. I remember standing on the toilet seat watching my dad use the medicine cabinet mirror and another mirror propped behind him to trim his hair, beard and mustache. I was in awe at how perfect all of his lines were! I couldn't wait to grow facial hair like him. Those days in the mirror gleaning lessons from him when he would say, "You know son, no matter what you do, stay clean."

"OK dad!"

Watching him groom to perfection just to run an errand made me realize how important it is for a man to take care of himself. I thought back to those days sitting in a booth at The Hamburger House listening to him tell his friends how overjoyed he was when he found out he was having a son.

"Yeah man, I knew it was going to be a boy because I was wearin' my cowboy boots!"

All of the men cracked up laughing and came by our table and gave my dad a high five. I had visions of my dad walking around in cowboy boots until I was born, but when I got older I realized that wasn't the case.

Now I am a college graduate, an employee of the FBI, applying to medical school, and feeling less confident because of this call. It was as if I were a child again, but it was just a few minutes ago. My mind came back to that conversation with my dad when I was ten and I told him that I could no longer be with him, and that he had to get his life together in order for me to be a part of it. On this day I had the opportunity to save my dad. I remember thinking, if I ever had the chance to help him I would be successful in doing so. God has now presented me with the opportunity.

I quickly came to the realization that in order for me to heal and reach the level of success I was striving for, I had to forgive and serve my father. There are many things I learned being a Christian and one of the most powerful is the power of forgiveness. Christianity has shown me four important lessons that God needs each of us to learn and practice: Salvation, Service, Restoration and Forgiveness. Only God can save us from ourselves through His Son, Jesus Christ. We are all commissioned to a life of service in that we should help our fellow man, regardless of what he looks like. Our job as Christians is to do our best to help restore everyone that has fallen. Truth be told, who hasn't fallen at least once and needed a helping hand?

Forgiveness is the most powerful tool God has given us, it breaks hate and drives out darkness.

To forgive someone is not easy. When faced with the opportunity to forgive, the power rests in your hands and in your heart. Now, that power was in my hands.

"Yes Dad, where are you? I'll come get you."

I've had thousands of people watch me on "stage" and applaud my performances. I've had just as many in the bleachers watch me play sports. All I ever cared about was one person who is the most important spectator I will ever have. The one person who I wanted to see me on stage and on the field, and never had—my dad, and now he is giving me a standing ovation.

I quickly called my mother and broke the news to her. I didn't have much time and we had to think fast. I called my two sisters as well. We decided that the best decision was to have dad stay with me. Dad had burned too many bridges with my sisters to consider staying with either of them. He had left a great woman with two daughters and a son with no relief, resources or answers. They were all ready to forgive as I was, but the forgetting part would be a lot more difficult.

I am now a twenty-three-year old man, the youngest of three children, in a position to help a man who barely helped me. I knew that I had to help for his benefit as well as my own. I asked my sister if she would drive with me to pick him up and she agreed. When we arrived in Atlantic City dad was where he said he would be. For the first time in many years dad made a promise and he kept it! I didn't realize how much I missed my dad until seeing him again on that day. He looked thin and frail. He carried a couple of green army duffle bags as if he was a soldier returning from war. Those bags contained all of his possessions, stories, and answers to dozens of questions that I had. I couldn't wait to open the bag to dad's life and find out what happened and why. All of that had to be put on hold, however, as this current moment was filled with the joy of seeing a man who I didn't know if I would ever see again. I could tell that life had been rough for him and wished that he hadn't gone through what he did. I thought about the things that must've happened to him and I felt bad. I knew that dad would be safe now, back with his family where he belonged.

We hugged a good hug.

"Dad."

"Hello son."

That was good enough for me.

ROLE REVERSAL

"We never know the love of a parent until we become parents ourselves."

- Henry Ward Beecher

Dad moved in and I made it clear that things were a little different now. Since he missed out on his opportunity to be dad, it was my turn to be the dad. I literally said, "Listen up dad, I'm the dad now, so just listen to what I have to say and we'll get along fine."

"OK son."

Yes, I had forgiven him, but I wanted it to be clear that living with me was on a trial run. I wasn't sure if he was still suffering from any addictions or in danger of relapsing. Luckily for me, I had nothing of real value in my apartment. Dad hadn't built a level of trust just yet so I had to be careful. I let him know that he had to abide by my rules:

Rule #1: No key.

Rule #2: Get up when I get up.

Rule #3: Leave when I leave.

Rule #4: If I call the VA Hospital and you're not there, don't come home!

At first, I thought I may have been a little rough on him but I soon realized that in order for him to become healthy, "tough" was what he required. Surprisingly, he agreed with all of these demanding rules because he was finally serious about turning his life around. Some things are easier said than done. The first couple of weeks were tough for dad. Neither of us slept much as he paced the floor back and forth. I stayed awake praying for his recovery. A healing had to take place both spiritually and physically and we were in the beginning stages. A toll had been taken on his body and mind and recovery was going to be a long and drawn-out process. I witnessed him dumping the many years of abuse into the toilet and not being able to help. A pat on the back or words of encouragement at that moment wasn't what he needed. Dad needed clinical therapy to make a transition into a clean and healthy lifestyle. I was not equipped to provide this sort of help but I knew who could.

My sisters and I placed him in an outpatient day program at the VA Hospital. Later, we realized that the risk of backsliding and access to drugs in the streets of Washington, DC was a reality, so we shifted our focus to an inpatient program. We identified The Harbor Light Salvation Army in Washington, DC. We had a lengthy conversation with the counselors at Harbor Light before we agreed to let our dad stay with them for his recovery.

"You have to understand that my father can talk his way in and out of anything. He is a very smooth man and before you know it, he can walk right out of this facility."

"I understand Mr. Mitchell."

"His recovery is paramount to our family. We need him well. We have a lot of catching up to do. We all believe that he has great purpose and destiny he has yet to fulfill.

"Mr. Mitchell you have my full confidence that we will do all that we can for your father. We deal with recovering addicts all the time and I have seen so many cases that I honestly have lost count. Your father will be well taken care of. I give you my word."

With that, my father was admitted to Harbor Light. At the same time, I was applying to medical school. I had to maintain my confidence because I was in the interview stage of the application process. I traveled to the schools that I applied to and interviewed for a spot in their program. I didn't have the luxury of taking time off to deal with personal matters. I knew at this point in my life I had to step up and be a man. This was my time.

"Some people want it to happen,
some people wish it would happen,
others make it happen."

- Michael Jordan

In my application process, I was getting all my ducks in a row. As I was setting myself up to be accepted and enter medical school, I applied to a Biotechnology Masters' Program at the Johns Hopkins University as a backup—in case I wasn't accepted into medical school the first time around. I applied to Howard University's School of Medicine, as well as The New Jersey Medical School in Newark. Not only was I accepted at Johns Hopkins for the Masters' Program, but I was also accepted into the New Jersey Medical School.

My transformation to medical school began at the same time as my father's transformation to sobriety. We were both on a mission to activate our faith and allow God to make the changes in our lives that we prayed for; dad to be drug-free and me to do well in medical school. This is what a typical day for both of us looked like:

6 AM

Roger Sr. - Shower and make bed. Clean dorm room.
Roger Jr. - Shower and review notes from previous lecture.

7 AM

Roger Sr. - Breakfast in cafeteria, then 30 minutes free time.
Roger Jr. - Breakfast at local coffee shop.

8 AM

Roger Sr. - Group therapy.
Roger Jr. - Meet study group and review notes.

9 AM

Roger Sr. - Meet with individual counselor.
Roger Jr. - Attend lectures: anatomy, biochemistry, microbiology.

1 PM

Roger Sr. - Lunch then .30 minutes free time.
Roger Jr. - Lunch then .30 minutes free time and review notes.

3 PM

Roger Sr. - Reading Bible in dorm room.
Roger Jr. - Sitting in cadaver lab dissecting donated body.

6 PM

Roger Sr. - Dinner. Visit from outside agency like AA. Back to dorm, laundry, free time and lights out 9 PM.
Roger Jr. - Dinner. Review notes. Study with partners until midnight.

6 AM

Roger Sr. - Same routine begins - 6 months.
Roger Sr. Same routine begins - 1st year.

Slowly the addiction lost its grip on my father and he began living, breathing and thinking again. It was not an overnight recovery by any stretch of the imagination, but it was a great start. As a first year medical student in my home state of New Jersey, I wasn't able to physically check-in on dad daily, but I was updated on his progress from my sisters and the counselors. I cannot tell you how many times I prayed, asking God to protect my father and bring him home. After five years with no results, I had all but lost hope. I still prayed, but I wasn't sure if my prayers were empty words or really reaching a God who heals any illness, disease or addiction. After 13 years, God answered my prayers! He proved to me and everyone else involved that He is all-powerful and loving. He brought my father back and was turning his life around right before our eyes. My hope was renewed as I clearly saw that restoration was possible and it began with my father.

My dad was overjoyed to be free from addiction. He says that being set free is difficult to explain to someone who has never been bound, but it is a feeling like none other. My father was able to become a father and friend to me. This was the man that I

lost so many years ago. This was what I had missing in my life. I had a void that I was calling out for, and now it was being filled. My father also had a void that he was filling with drugs and alcohol. Now that he was delivered from the poison of those substances, he started going to church.

Dad found something in the church that he had been looking for all his life. What he was searching for was not at the end of a blunt or at the bottom of a glass. It was not at the end of a crack pipe. He was looking for unconditional love and a relationship with Jesus Christ. God's love allowed him to love himself. Christianity filled the void that he had and his heart changed. Dad read the Bible and other self-help and inspirational books. He became so immersed in his Christian walk that the counselors at Harbor Light admired him. They elevated him from being a patient to being a mentor to younger recovering addicts. My dad gladly accepted his new role as he didn't want to see any other young man or woman go through what he did. He participated in groups, and fellowshipped both inside and outside of the church. Dad possessed an energetic zeal for God that I hadn't seen since my days in the Thompson home, many years ago. What a blessing to see my dad truly born again.

Not long after my dad began mentoring young people, he identified an opportunity to work as a janitor at the VA Hospital. He applied and was accepted to work in a simple work release program. His job was to clean floors and toilets, and he

was totally fine with it. Roger Mitchell Sr. was a man now in his late fifties and had seen the world. He owned several businesses and homes. He had many nice cars and dressed in the latest fashion, and his pockets were always lined with cash. He had been an accomplished man, but now was using toothbrushes to clean grout around urinal stalls and doing it with a humility that I had never seen.

Still eager to serve while he was working in the VA Hospital, he learned about a substance abuse ward that was in need of counselors. He applied and worked his way into the position as a Substance Abuse Counselor. He was now in a place where he could share his testimony and his recovery with men just like him. Dad really wanted to share the importance of sobriety. He had moved up the ranks from janitor to counselor and was really helping men. I couldn't be any prouder of him. As I was working to come into my own destiny, my dad was working to move into his. Neither of us was aware that the paths we were currently on were God's chosen path for us many years ago. More importantly, I didn't realize that the forgiveness I was now extending towards my father was more for me than it was for him.

True forgiveness is a release. It is letting go of toxins similar to any drugs or alcohol a person uses to escape life's pressures. If you hold on to bitterness in your heart, you are slowly killing yourself just as with cocaine or heroin.

The lasting effects of drug abuse are devastating. There is a necessary healing and recovery process for the abuser and the entire family. Just as God worked on my father's heart while he was in rehab, God worked on my heart to forgive a father who walked out on me. Now that God brought him back into my life, I had no choice but to wholeheartedly forgive him because God did what I specifically asked him to do. When my father asked me for forgiveness I knew he was sincere.

"Dad, I forgive you and I love you."

Those words released me to continue along the journey towards the man I was becoming. I believe they released me to be the father I am today. Where fear once existed in my heart now forgiveness resides. With my newfound freedom in forgiveness I could pursue the next phase of ultimate success for my life. Fear was dead.

"The weak can never forgive.
Forgiveness is the attribute of the strong."

- Mahatma Gandhi

Chapter Thirteen

HEEDING THE CALL

"For I know the plans I have for you," declares the Lord "plans to prosper you and not to harm you, plans to give you hope and a future."

- Jer. 29:11

EVER since I realized that God was my Father I remained in constant communication with Him. I found myself in a place of declarations. I made promises to God in order to get to the place that I wanted to be—medical student and successfully matriculate at Howard. Since God already made that happen, I knew He had the power to make my next pursuit also happen. In any negotiation there are two parties. In my case, it was God and me.

"God if you get me into medical school, I will give my life to you. I will abstain from behavior that can be damaging to me. God, I know you have the power to get me into medical school. God if you do this for me, I will no longer indulge in mind-altering substances. God, please give me the chance to be challenged. Give me the opportunity to prove that Howard has prepared me and I have prepared myself. Give me the chance to be better than I currently am. Give me the chance to be the physician that I longed to be."

I had a Fisher Price stethoscope and medical kit as a child. At seven years old the vision began forming in my mind that I wanted to be a physician. I ran around the house listening to my mother and sister's heartbeat. I wouldn't take the stethoscope off. I always had the reflex hammer in my pocket and tried to get people to let me check their reflexes. Sixteen years have now passed and I lay in bed, praying that God continues to guide my path to achieving my desire that is so close I can smell it.

"Before I formed you in the womb I knew you,
before you were born I set you apart..."
                                        - Jer. 1:5

When I received the notification that I had been accepted into New Jersey Medical School. I was both elated and grateful because a childhood dream was coming to pass. God had answered both the prayer for my father's recovery and the prayer of my desire in life. I thanked God and told Him that I would uphold my end of the bargain. I told Him of the changes that I would make in my life and I was not going to back down on what I had said. God kept His end, I would now do my part and diligently keep mine. This was more than a passion or desire for me. This was my calling to walk into. It was something that was bigger than me before I was born. I didn't have a choice in accepting what God was doing in my life.

DOCTORS ORDERS

Being a physician was a personal dream since I could remember, but it also placed me into a lineage within my family that I wanted to be included in. It was almost like looking at a college fraternity from the outside. The fraternity guys wear their jackets, sing fraternity songs, and know the fraternity secrets. Only members have these privileges. It is an exclusive membership that many people are diligently trying to gain access to. This is how I felt in regard to the other physicians in my family. The doctors in my family were a bonded brotherhood that I desperately wanted to join. I wanted to continue a legacy of great achievers who served their families and communities through medicine.

My grandfather was one of the first Black physicians in Atlantic

City. He was well respected and revered in the community as well as within the brotherhood of his colleagues in medicine, politics and entertainment. My Uncle Byron told me stories of those days when Black entertainers, politicians or athletes traveled through Atlantic City for conferences, meetings or shows. They had two options for overnight lodging: either stay in the Negro quarters that were substandard or stay with my grandparents who owned a modest home on Indiana Avenue. My grandparents were accustomed to allowing prominent Blacks to stay with them. Their guests ranged from the likes of performers like Duke Ellington and Count Basie to Prizefighter Jersey Woe Walcott. I recall my grandfather telling me exciting stories about his guests over the years and I looked forward to hearing each one.

Everyone is called to something by God. Your assignment as you journey through your life is to find out what that assignment is and then perform it.

Mark Twain once said, "The two most important days of your life are the day you are born and the day you find out why." I remember as a child going into stores with my mother in Atlantic City and people stopped her on the street and said to me,

"Your grandfather, Dr. Marshall delivered me!"

"Your grandfather was my doctor!"

"I loved your grandfather!"

My grandmother told me how my grandfather accepted pies and cakes as payment for patient services. That would always frustrate her because she knew they needed the money.

I was also fortunate to have my Uncle Donald who was an emergency room physician in Washington DC. He attended Howard University for undergraduate studies and then went on to Georgetown University for medical school. He is my mother's brother and always set an example for fatherhood, manhood, and professional service.

I've always been the type of person to draw motivation and inspiration from a variety of places. I believe motivation can be drawn and fuel you into whatever it is you wish to pursue. Now, I was preparing to embark on the most important journey of my life. To date, I had accomplished amazing things that many people don't have the opportunity nor resources to accomplish. Yet the task that lay ahead of me was larger and grander than all the previous ones.

I'll never forget the night I got the phone call. I was home from work at the FBI and I was ready to prepare for dinner. The phone rang.

"Hello, may I speak to Roger Mitchell?"

"This is Roger. Who am I speaking with?"

"This is Dr. Heinrich from the New Jersey Medical School, University of Medicine and Dentistry of New Jersey."

I thought back to opening my acceptance letter to Howard University. At the time, it was the most important moment of my life. That event is now years in my rear view mirror and now I am faced with the same feeling. I could feel the small hairs on the back of my neck stand at attention. My heart was beating so loud it felt like it was coming through my chest. Or did my chest just come out of my throat? Time stopped. With my voice cracking, I responded.

"Yes sir. How may I help you?"

"I have the unique opportunity to call the accepted students into the New Jersey Medical School."

I literally paused. Was he talking about me? For a brief moment, I considered the fact that he could be calling to give me the bad news that I had NOT been accepted.

"Dr. Mitchell. Congratulations! You have been accepted into the New Jersey School of Medicine and Dentistry!"

This was the first time anyone has ever referred to me as "Dr. Mitchell" and the sound of it blew me off my feet. It felt official now.

I hadn't sat for one day of medical school, yet he referred to me as "Dr. Mitchell." Those words would forever permeate my consciousness. My excitement lasted through my registration period, buying books, and all of the other preliminary things I had to get done in order to start. I looked at different ways I could be successful in medical school. What would it take? What would I need to do differently? What did I have to prepare for?

I had been out of school for two years. I entered the working world after my graduation from Howard. Although that world gave me perspective and preparation to a certain extent, I had to retrain myself to a lifestyle of long hours of intense studying. I felt I was ready when the pre-matriculation program began. This is a program that starts before the actual first semester begins. The program gives you a taste of medical school and what you can expect. Although this is a valuable program, nothing can prepare you for the rigors of what medical school is really like. I've heard an accurate analogy to medical school in that it's like a person being told to drink directly from an open and active fire hydrant at full blast. Some people may approach this challenge by standing directly in front of the shooting stream of water with a wide open mouth hoping to consume every drop. They will quickly find themselves choking, wet, and lying on their back. Some may grab a cup and stand to the side to fill it up and sip their way through. I took the approach of standing to the side, staying dry, and sipping long and hard with a straw to fill my mind with knowledge. Actually, there is no way for a medical student to get it all—it's just too much volume, coming at you so fast, and under intense pressure.

There were times where I thought that each professor must have forgotten that they were not the only instructor that we had. There was so much information for one course that it left little time to study for another course. A normal day was at least 20 hours' worth of work. Between classes during the day, labs in the afternoon, and studying at night, it left little room for sleep, let alone eat. Medical school classes and undergraduate classes aren't the same. Both are challenging. Both will set you up for a career in medicine. One will lay the foundation and the other will build upon it. Nonetheless, if you enter medical school with the same study techniques that were successful for you in college, you may not succeed. A different depth of commitment is necessary. Those that get this and understand it quickly are more apt to succeed overall.

None of these issues bothered me. I had prepared myself for the rigors of medical school since I had been hearing about them for years. My grandfather, a man of many stories, had secured in my mind the dedication and commitment that a medical school education would entail. This is not where my failure came. My failure was in my belief that my two years as a forensic biologist with the FBI would somehow negate my need for serious and intense study. I felt that I knew all that I needed to know about the science of DNA. I believed that the knowledge I had gained on the job would be enough with minimal study in medical school. As a result of this thinking, I failed my Genetics final exam because I didn't study for it! I had to retake it. Thankfully I passed.

I took for granted my knowledge-base in the classroom and I failed my first two board exams as well. This was a huge disappointment for me as I was both crushed and embarrassed. The board exams are serious stepping stones in medical school. Students who don't pass the Board Exams seldom matriculate successfully. If you don't have a grasp of the concepts of medicine enough to pass the boards, this may be the rude awakening that this industry is just not for you. This thinking however never entered my mind. I never thought of quitting. I thought I told you that I won't stop...

Although the Board Examination was a wakeup call and as much as it hurt me to fail, my thoughts and lifestyle hadn't improved. Therefore, I failed a second exam of similar importance. That exam was the last exam that I failed. This is where my true turnaround came. I realized that my performance was directly linked to my decisions. My success was interwoven with my choices. It became crystal clear to me that I had been taking this incredible opportunity for granted and resting on what I considered to be enough head-knowledge to pass.

The environment you place yourself in will directly correlate with the outcomes you wish to achieve. If you seek academic success, you cannot spend your entire day hanging out with friends. Instead you have to use your time wisely and prepare yourself for real world success.

It took me failing to learn this. The greatest lessons in life are not what makes you fall on your butt. Instead, it is the inner strength that it takes for you to get back up. This was the epiphany and small nugget of truth that freed me from my former way of thinking. From that moment moving forward, I never failed another exam. What I took away from that time in my life are these words that have become the cornerstone of the man I am today: Truth, Faith, and Choices. These words now anchor me and are the pillars to my foundation.

Failure never equates to quitting. Only quitting equates to quitting. I had too much of a legacy, a destiny and a purpose to throw in the towel. I never let failing an exam stop me. I used it for fuel and motivation. I saw it as a distraction and a hurdle, but every hurdle is built to be jumped over. I jumped with all that I had and I landed square on my feet.

THE LEGACY CONTINUES

My legacy is strong. Not only because of the work done by my grandparents on my mother's side of the family but also due to the strength of character of my grandfather on my father's side. I loved to hear stories about how strong Grandpa Buddy was. He worked for Bethlehem Steel his entire life. To me he was a giant at five- feet-five inches. As a child, I saw how he handled steel and bent steel bars with his bare hands, like Superman. He was also strong-willed and had strong opinions. He was upright and righteous. It was through his stories that I learned to be a strong man and a leader of my future family. Grandpa Buddy only had a seventh grade education yet he vowed that all of his kids would go to college. Both of his daughters went to college and my dad chose the military. Grandpa Buddy taught me how to fight because he was a Golden Gloves fighter in the Army. He gave me my first jump rope with the wooden handles and the boxer wraps that went around my hands. Whenever I faced what I considered adversity in my own life, I often conjured up my grandfather's stories of strength.

Chapter Fourteen

FAITH AND FAMILY

"I prefer to be true to myself, even at the hazard of incurring the ridicule of others, rather than to be false, and to incur my own abhorrence."

- Frederick Douglass

MEDICAL school is like taking off in an airplane. When the plane first takes off, there is a lot of speed needed for the plane to lift off the ground. There is momentum, force and velocity. When the nose of the plane rises, the thrust of the engines are at full blast. When the wings cut through the air and the plane enters the sky, the sheer power of the takeoff causes each person to lean back in their seat. The takeoff is such a powerful part of the trip that you are not allowed to stand. It is rocky and turbulent. The takeoff is both loud and outstanding. This is how I felt when medical school started. Most medical school students will probably agree with this analogy. Once you settle in however, the medical school experience settles in as an airplane does. When an airplane reaches a certain altitude, it will be placed on cruise control. By the time I was in my second year of medical school it was as if I could hear the captain's voice over the intercom telling me, "Roger, you are free to walk about the cabin." I secured the best study methods, sleep patterns, and learning habits to succeed.

At this point in my matriculation, my thoughts were no longer concerned with making it through exams and surviving. I did not spend so much time focusing on taking a drink from an exploding fire hydrant. I thought about a scripture I came across very early in the Bible. Genesis (2:18), says that "it is not good for man to be alone." Realizing this, I knew I had to join myself with the woman of my dreams. I had to have someone in my life whom I could build a future. I wanted to share it with a special person whom I could be honest and loyal to.

It had been a few years since Angelique Hendricks and I had dated. We had gone our separate ways since our days of meeting in chemistry class at Howard. Although she had made a definite impression on me, I was enjoying the freedom of being a single male in medical school, and wanted to party like a rock star. For a time, I dated numerous women, drank, and went against the very promise I made to God. He has a way however, of reminding us of who we are. God will show you what He has placed in you and what your destiny will be if we follow and obey Him. I was continuously reminded that I could do better and that I could be better. I made a decision that the stability of a committed relationship was one of the thing I lacked yet needed. I called Angie and through our brief conversation, I quickly learned how never to approach a woman.

"Hey Angie, its Rog." I said confidently.

"Hi Roger. How are you?" she replied.

"I'm good. Listen, I'm getting out of the game and since you and I are such good friends, I'm going to give you a chance."

As a 27 year old, this was a very arrogant statement for me to make. It made it seem as if I thought that I was the best thing since sliced bread, or as my dad says, "all that and a bag of beans!" Angie quickly put me in my place.

"What makes you think I want to settle down with you?"

Her question silenced me. I wasn't expecting her question but as I look back on it, it is a question that suggests the inner workings of a successful marriage. Marriage is about balance. It isn't about one person ruling over the other person. It isn't about one person succumbing to the other person.

Provision is the most important element in regard to how a man is to see his family. The true test of a man is whether he handles his responsibilities with no excuses. Provision is not limited to material things although those things are important.

So, as a third year medical student, did I understand all of this? Was I willing to contemplate the necessary questions? What is manhood? What did manhood mean to me? If I had a desire to settle down and be married, I had to define for myself what manhood was. Not only define it, but exemplify it in my thoughts and actions. Angie's response to my awkward question challenged me. It made me seriously run through all of these questions and definitions in my mind. I realized that I had to reassess and define these things for myself and be prepared to come at her correct. So as a starving medical student, I pulled together a little bit of money and sent her flowers with a note, asking her out on a date. She was gracious enough to give me a second chance. I traveled down from New Jersey to Washington, DC and took Angie on a date in Georgetown. We sat and discussed what it would be like to reconnect. It didn't take long through the dating process for me to recognize that dating wouldn't be enough. I knew that I had to marry Angelique. So I asked. This time I asked the proper way; without the arrogance and haughtiness, and with the vision of my role as a man. Angie's answer this time was more to my liking. She said "yes."

I don't believe I have ever smiled as hard as I did on that sunny day August 31st, 2002. We got married at New Bethel Baptist Church on 9th and S Streets NW, in Washington, DC. It was a beautiful wedding. My friends and family attended. Both mine and Angelique's grandmothers were there. Both of them are no longer with us. It was a full circle day for me as my father attended. The day couldn't have been better. The wedding exceeded our expectations, although we didn't have much money to have an extravagant wedding. One of the highlights of the wedding reception was when the toasts were given. Friends and family all stood with glasses full of sparkling cider (we were in the basement of the church, so sparkling cider was the allowed beverage) and offered words of encouragement, advice, and love to Angie and me. Angie's cousin took her turn and raised her glass to us. She then offered words to the happy bride and groom.

"...and Angie is so beautiful! No one would have known that she is four months pregnant!"

The looks on people's faces were astonished. My new bride and I shared a glance and a smile that was classic. To this day, we recollect that moment and smile. There was surprised looks as everyone was taken aback. There quickly became cause for celebration for two reasons. One celebrating us as bride and groom, and now they could celebrate our expectant a child. We were overjoyed!

Earlier, when I found out that the love of my life was pregnant, I immediately knew that I had to marry Angie. Not out of obligation for I was going to marry her anyway. I loved this woman. Rather, it was important to me that my son have my last name. I know how it is for men who fathered children unmarried. I know how they are treated by doctors and nurses in hospitals. I know how Black men in general are regarded when they are unwed fathers. The perception is that they will not be good fathers nor own up to their responsibilities. It is also believed that the mother will raise the child alone. This was not going to be my story. I would not be defined by what society or anyone else thinks. My concern for my life is what God thinks about me. My aim was to please God. I knew at the moment of learning that Angie was pregnant with my child that I would be the dad that I always wanted. I knew that I would never abandon my son or any of my children. I made a promise to God first, to Angie, to my unborn son and to myself that I would be the provider and protector that they needed. It was my duty to Angie and my duty to my son.

For me, it's impossible to separate my manhood from my fatherhood. Manhood and fatherhood are interchangeable but difficult to separate for real men. If you can imagine trying to separate water from wetness or tall from height—you can't do it. That is how I see manhood and fatherhood.

You can become a man without necessarily becoming a father; but you cannot become a father without becoming a man.

My firstborn son, Nathaniel, arrived when I was a fourth year student in medical school. We call him the G.O.A.T. (Greatest of All Time). He is an intellectually precocious child. We saw at a very young age that he was ahead of his peers in terms of his mental capabilities. My second child Nina is very sensitive and sweet. She is artistic and also shares intellectual advancements with her brothers. Her love-language is different than my sons. Our youngest son Matthew has been given the nickname 'Baby Africa.' Matthew was diagnosed with Glucose 6 Phosphate Dehydrogenase Deficiency. This is an alteration of his red blood cells which makes him more protected against malaria. He is practically immune to the malarial disease but it also makes his red blood cells more fragile. This places him at risk for anemia. His form seems to have originated in Africa, hence, the nickname that we affectionately gave him. Matthew probably understands himself better than his other siblings and has shown himself capable of charting his own course even at seven years old.

Each of my children model the behavior of myself and my wife. With that, I understand the great responsibility that lies with me as a father. I have to take on the responsibility of being a father who is present and intentional. I have to be careful what I say and do in my home because my children will mimic what they see. Yet the most important and vital thing that I learned in this entire process is that as a father, I have to draw from my relationship with God in order to relate and conduct my fatherly duties as a man. My wife will follow my lead as I am obedient and follow God's lead. My children will mimic my example as I attempt to live a righteous life after God. This is the protocol that God wants for the family. This is how I live my life today.

GRABBING THE YELLOW ROSE

When I understood myself through a true submission to God it became so important for me to live my life in as righteous a manner as I could. I now had a wife, a family and starting a career. I was maturing in God and was navigating out of my residency. We found ourselves making the decision to move my family to Houston, Texas. I wasn't sure why I was supposed to go there, but for some reason I felt led to do so. I had an opportunity to work as a medical examiner in the Harris County Institute of Forensic Sciences, which was very exciting. My wife and I had never lived outside of the east coast. I had a distant cousin from my father's side who lived there so I had some family. My wife and I set out on a journey. My youngest son, Baby Africa, was just born and we began looking for a home in a suburb of Houston. The baby was only one month old when we took the flight to Houston.

My wife and I visited 16 houses in two days. After the exhausting process, we chose a beautiful home, unlike any we had ever had seen. Previous to this move, we had rented and even stayed with family members. Our house was a 3,300 square-foot brick home with five bedrooms, three bathrooms and a detached garage. Neither Angie nor I had ever lived in a home that big. We were excited. I will never forget the look on my wife's face when we settled on this. We felt ready to take on the world! We were a young couple with 3 small children and we were very happy.

Now there was one thing lacking that left me with a feeling of being incomplete. I needed to find a new church home. I was doing everything else. I had a budding career and was going to my children's games, yet I was not spiritually anchored. We visited churches and we were fortunate to find a church called Harvest of Praise Exalted (HOPE). After walking into that church, it was clear that I had been missing something in my spiritual relationship. I truly submitted to God. In doing so, my entire family submitted. My wife began to see clearer and my children followed. This was also when I began to experience when true freedom and forgiveness came. I had cried out to God in previous years and I had forgiven my father. Yet at the age of 35, when I committed to submission and the Lordship of God, I learned a valuable lesson. I learned that your freedom and your hearts desires are directly related to your faith. Your faith also allows you to discover your personal pursuits and what is important to you. A double-minded man is unstable in all his ways (James 1:8). Therefore, if you seek to cause confusion and chaos, you will find it as it ties in to your faith.

THE CROSSROAD

I had officially been a resident of Texas for less than one year. Things were going very well. I had a wonderful career and a loving family. We had found a great church that was pouring into us and we were growing. The children were doing well in school and Angie and I were involved parents. They had sports and other activities and we were supportive. I know the feeling of looking for my dad so I made sure my son never had to look for me. When he turned toward the bleachers, he saw me. If my daughter looked out into the crowd, she saw me. If Angie needed me, I was there. If I needed Angie, she was there. One would think that I had the perfect scenario and for all purposes, it was. There was only one thing that bothered me and

I could not shake it no matter how hard I tried. I wanted to go back to the east coast. I realized that I had moved away from all that I knew. I had moved far from my family in terms of my parents and my sister. One of my sisters actually did move to Texas, but my other sister was still back east. I always called the east home.

I began looking for jobs on the east coast and not too long into my search, I saw an open position that peaked my interest. The job was in Washington, DC at the Office of the Chief Medical Examiner. I had worked there as a chief resident in the past and knew some of the staff. The prospect of returning to the DC area excited me. Of course both Angie and I attended college in Washington so there was a familiarity. I could easily consider DC home as it wasn't far from my hometown in New Jersey. I excitedly applied and was granted a phone interview. The interview went well and I was offered the job.

At the same time that I'm faced with these life altering choices, a position opened in Harris County, Texas for the Assistant Deputy Chief Medical Examiner in charge of all death investigations for the county. This was a tremendous opportunity for advancement and growth in my career. A position like this would cause me to consider staying. What floated through my mind with this opportunity was the feeling that I wasn't as experienced as some of the other applicants and if I applied for this position, I would be turned away. Yet I heard a voice that indicated to me that this job was available. I had a choice to make. I approached Angie to get her feelings on the matter.

"Angie I have a decision to make and I'm at a crossroads. A position is available in DC in the Office of the Chief Medical Examiner. I think I want it. I want to go back home. I miss being out east with my mom. You know my dad is there and I miss him too."

"Rog I'm not ready to move back to the east coast yet. You said we'd be here for 5 years. I like our church. I like my friends. I'm not ready to go. The kids aren't ready to go."

Do I pursue the east which I was longing for? Do I uproot the family against the wishes of my wife? Do I stay and apply for a job which I feel is beyond my experience?

I applied for the position in Texas and I got the job over candidates who I thought were more qualified than me. I made a choice to stay and took a leap of faith and it worked out in my favor. Now in a year's time, I was promoted to run a staff of 24 and a budget of 2.2 million dollars. As a mid-level manager, I learned what it took to manage a unit within a large organization.

Every choice you make has an outcome. Put on your boots of rightly related choices and lace them up! If you choose to smoke a pack of cigarettes a day, that choice may lead to emphysema. If you choose to drink a fifth of liquor a day, that choice may lead to liver failure. These choices I've made transitioned me to a place of a deeper relationship with God.

Chapter Fifteen

A VOICE FOR THE VOICELESS

"There are things you stand up for because it's right."

- Nikki Giovanni

I'LL never forget an event that changed my life. I was a first year medical student watching the news I saw a story about Amadou Diallo, a twenty-something year old immigrant man from Africa. He was on his way home and was confronted by several members of the New York Police Department. They questioned him and asked to see his hands. In a nervous state and not sure what to do, he reached into his pocket. This young man was not well-versed on the African-American culture and our relationship with law enforcement. He had never been told how to respond if he were ever to be questioned by an officer. Reaching into his pocket, he pulled out his wallet. He was trying to show identification to the police. Before he was able to get his wallet out the officers opened fire. He sustained multiple gunshot wounds. Shot after shot, his body toiled around in the vestibule of his New York apartment. Shots ricocheted off the concrete sidewalk as they pierced and destroyed his skin surface. His clothing was drenched in blood, tears and sweat. He was propped up like a mannequin on his front door, shot to death nineteen times.

It was clear that there was a racial disparity here. In my life, I can remember being profiled in West Windsor, New Jersey. I was walking with a group of Black friends and was told to sit on the curb until I was questioned. I was patted down with my hands on a wall and forced to answer questions. All the while I was thinking, "Would this be happening if my friends and I were white?" My only crime that night was making a decision to walk through downtown Princeton, New Jersey.

Although I had dealt with this situation and others of racism in my life, there was something about this event that was different for me. Being in medical school with the intent on being a medical examiner, this case that I saw on TV hit me hard. It hit me in my heart and in my conscious. It rendered me both breathless and speechless. There was something about Amadou Diallo. I found out that he had bullet entrance wounds on the soles of his feet. These are wounds that any man who was being perceived as a threat to law enforcement should not have. He received these injuries while lying on his back, where he would no longer be a threat. The number of bullets that entered his body well surpassed the point of necessary force.

I began researching law enforcement and unusual force. I talked to other physicians who had also taken a stand for social responsibility. I attended trainings on torture and researched the findings. I learned about post-traumatic stress disorder and how it works with torture. I learned how violent behavior was often a symptom of exposure to violence. This reinforced the work I had been doing at the FBI and at the Student National Medical Association.

Not long after the death of Diallo and close to home in Essex County, New Jersey, there was another shooting homicide involving law enforcement and a young black man. This time however, the victim of the shooting was a female police officer. This terrible event caused a task force to be created to find the killer. Several Black men were detained and arrested in an effort to identify the killer. Several men were abused in their homes with their civil rights compromised. Earl Faison fit the description of the killer. He was brought in as a possible suspect and was beaten badly once in police custody.

He was both beaten and sprayed with pepper spray. With asthma as his underlying condition, he died due to the nature of his injuries. The manner of death was established as undetermined.

As a first year medical student and someone who is extremely concerned with social advocacy, I found fault in that conclusion. Although I hadn't been trained in forensic medicine, I still disagreed with that diagnosis. This upset me. I felt enraged. My recourse was to take to the streets with other concerned citizens. I felt compelled to join the masses who gathered to let their voices and opinions be heard. It was later determined that Earl Faison wasn't the killer. Even if Earl Faison was the killer, he never received his day in court. There was another Black man killed needlessly—another life stolen.

It became clear to me that excessive law enforcement force was a public health issue. I identified through research conducted by the Department of Justice (DOJ) and the Bureau of Justice Statistics (BJS) that police contact with African-Americans were disproportionately high. Research found these statistics even higher in urban areas. I also identified that the practices of hog tying and choke holds being administered in South Africa during apartheid, yielded increased mortality and morbidity among the citizen victims. It became clear to me that forensic pathology and the medical examiner had a role and a responsibility to diagnose these cases correctly to ensure that the public had the proper discourse in a court of law.

Prosecutors should set out to prove the police criminally responsible for the death of a citizen during grand jury investigations. Often, many set out to prove that the use of deadly force was justified. Many of these cases never even make it to a court of law. This is not an easy issue to solve. Law enforcement is a peculiar institution in that it is empowered to use deadly force to resolve violent conflict. How can public opinion change for young Black men, young Hispanic men, and poor men? How can we encourage a balance of the force taken against these men? How can we improve the law enforcement and the criminal justice system when many of their cases never make it to trial?

I often say, "if all we had to worry about were the deaths caused by law enforcement in our community, then through advocacy, demonstration, and proper policy, we could end such death disparities." However, law enforcement is not the primary cause of gun violence in our community. The most important and demonstrative public health disparity surrounding black men in this country is gun violence. According to the Centers for Disease Control (CDC) the number one killer of Black males ranging in age from 10-35 is homicide. The number two killer of Hispanic males within that same age group is also homicide. Homicide is the number two cause of death for all adolescents only falling behind accidents. Suicides are rising among the adolescent community suffering from mental illnesses such as depression and anxiety. The common thread between the majority of homicides and suicides is that they occur at the end of the gun.

With killings of Michael Brown and Trayvon Martin, the active shooter killings at Sandy Hook Elementary, gun violence has received more attention in media. There is a definite need for individual education, policy enactment and control measures to ensure a decrease in this violent behavior.

Violence is a public health issue. It is the public health sector that continues to abdicate its responsibility to solve the problems of violence in our communities.

As many people say, we can't arrest ourselves out of the problems of violence in our communities. In other words, moving young brothers off of one block doesn't solve the greater issue of lack of access to jobs, vocational opportunities and adequate education. Merely moving the problem to another block is like placing a band aid on a bullet wound—as if the placement of the band aid is the solution. It is not! The band aid is a simple fix to a small cut, whereas a bullet wound is a major injury. A band aid does nothing but prolong and further the problem. The problem will become worse over time if not adequately treated.

It is imperative that we make these connections with all that is surrounding the children and youth in our communities with the threat of potential violence. We have to do all that we can to help identify and solve the problem. We shouldn't have to ask law enforcement to do that. Their job is to protect property and life. It is the responsibility of the public health sector to solve the problem of health disparity in these communities. Currently, the public health sector is abdicating its responsibility.

After a typical day as I drive home to my wife and children I reflect on how violence has claimed the lives of so many in our community. I have sat with countless families with tears in my eyes as they come to identify their loved ones. I cannot help but pray for every family and mourn their loss. Life is not a game. Do not take for granted the potential you have and what has been provided for you. Do not take for granted the things that are in front of you. There is a promise in your heart which will enable you to treat and serve others to help them become the best that they can be.

We all have the ability to serve. Make good choices and use your gifts to help others.

Chapter Sixteen

FRUITS OF A SUCCESSFUL FUTURE

"Thus, by their fruit you will recognize them."

- Matt. 7:20

MY journey has been highlighted by a myriad of events and special people. A tumultuous childhood lacking the emotional support of a father but filled with the love, care, and support of a nuclear and extended family. A family that was accomplished in education and the service of others which built a solid foundation for me. I had many examples of what success looked like. Whether it was the success of a beautiful and phenomenal artist in the form of my Aunt Betty, or a caring counselor in the form of Aunt Joan. I also value the financial leadership of my mother and looked to my grandfathers that stood as strong men and coverings for their families. I had uncles who loved their wives and children and neighbors who showed examples of Godliness. I was surrounded by a community of individuals who poured into me and tilled the soil around me as my seed was nurtured. The love that I had from these consistent adults acted as the foundation toward helping me identify that my purpose was in *service. The price of freedom is service.* There were times that I felt like I should give up. I had failed exams. I had missed the mark. I made promises to God and then went back on my word. All have sinned and fall short of the glory of God (Rom.

3:23). At the end of the day, I realize that my life was full of so much more abundance than lack. God has a way of supplying all that I needed.

Through it all, I found purpose to serve others. I had more of an affinity toward what could be accomplished by loving other people that I forgot about what I may have lacked. The relationships I developed with family members, friends, and colleagues are all nurtured in my purpose of service. Each of these categories of people, even those considered enemies, have played a key role in who I am. I had dreamt of being a forensic scientist physician, and forensic pathologist. My dreams became more and more specific as to who I would become. When I realized that my passion would interlock with my profession, I had to challenge and question myself. How could I use my profession to give a voice to the voiceless? How could I use my profession to ensure that there is justice and equality? How could I use my profession to show righteousness? How could my profession be a testimony?

Clarity of self is so critically important toward your development of your passion into purpose.

It's one thing to be passionate about something. Many of us are very passionate about our favorite sports teams. It's another thing to have a profession. A professional is nothing more than someone who gets paid to deliver a product or service. When you can interlock your passion with your profession, however, you can really change your life and the others around you.

What are you passionate about and how can you nurture your passion so it becomes part of what you do daily?

Knowing the next steps for myself, my family, and my career have been paramount to my success. One thing I realized in my journey is that knowing what you want to be when you grow up and being passionate about it won't get you there by itself. It merely sets the stage for your success. It is through hard work and dedication that you begin to create an environment that will allow your dreams to manifest into reality. If you want to be an educator, then school is your environment. If you want to be a basketball player, then the basketball court is your environment.

My wrong choices may always be present, so I teach my children how long-lasting the wrong choice can be. I teach them how judgmental the human spirit is and how the wrong choice can follow you for years to come. I also let them know that righteousness is not perfection. A man's righteousness is only through the God that he serves.

As I mentioned, I understand that the roadblock to many people's success is the fear of failure. Many are hindered by the fear of failing in the pursuit of what they are passionate about. This is a very real fear in the hearts of minds of millions of people. For me, I had a need for acceptance from a father who wasn't there. That need overshadowed my existence and empowered my fear of failure. I was already in a place where nothing could possibly hurt me more than I had already been hurt.

Whatever is placed in front of your pathway to purpose and success, make sure you do all that you can to travel down that road and achieve it.

Standing in who you are will allow you to make the right choice when no one around you is brave enough to do so. Standing out means you're standing up. You don't have to fear being alone. Stand up! It is important that you stand up and let the haters hate and let the naysayers say what they want. They will tell you that you are too young to be in leadership. They will tell you that you have the wrong skin color. They will tell you that you can't. By standing up, you are empowering yourself and everyone around you to succeed. Your success can be so contagious that even the haters and naysayers will succeed.

These are the keys to success that is sustainable through freedom, choices, and an unyielding compromise. You will then be able to plant seeds. By serving others and being invested in seeing others benefit from your actions, this yields fruit; it's planting seeds. I am harvesting fruit from the choice seeds I planted years ago. My choices have been these seeds. The principles of planting seeds so that they will grow and prosper and bear fruit are concepts that everyone must learn. Stop being scared of making the choices that will develop you into the person that you need to be. Stop being scared of your own success.

It is understood that fear plays a big part in our decision to make choices. It is important to put away your fears and make the choices that benefit you and your communities. Far too many times I see the result of people's bad choices lying on my autopsy table way too early. Don't be that wrong choice. Fear not and choose life!

At 37 years old, I became the Chief Medical Examiner for the

Northern Region of New Jersey. In that capacity, I also served as the Assistant State Medical Examiner in Charge. In that role, my responsibility was to oversee medical examiner operations for the state of New Jersey. To some of you reading this book, 37 is old. To others, 37 is young. It normally takes 10 years of practice to reach this level of responsibility. It took me 5 years. I was the youngest Chief Medical Examiner in any jurisdiction. The jurisdiction that covered Essex, Hudson, Passaic and Somerset Counties with cities such as Newark, Irvington, Jersey City, Patterson and others. My success was both rare and unheard of. I was humbled to be given this responsibility yet I hadn't felt the fullness of success until the point in which I could share my story. I have prayed that my story would be one that would allow individuals to potentially gain satisfaction based on their own success. I prayed that my story would help someone remove the barriers from what may be holding them back.

I got a phone call after two years in New Jersey that the Chief Medical Examiner position for a large metropolitan area was available. This was a very sought after position in our nation's capital. As the story in New Jersey ends, I stand before you now as a 40 year old Black man who was raised without a father, but now has a father as a best friend. I have been nurtured by a community who has loved me. I have strong relationships and friendships that will sustain me. I'm a husband and a father. I'm a son of a mother who is an angel. I'm a proud grandson of a legacy that has inspired me to attempt to be great. This is who I am! But this book is about you!

My mind goes back to the time I was thrown in the deep end by my father. There has not been a "deep end" that I have faced in my life that I have not heard the cheers of my family saying "you can do it!" I learned that being thrown into the deep end whether by loved ones or God makes me stronger in my ability to succeed. This book was written to encourage the notion that nothing is insurmountable and that you can win whether you have to journey alone or with the help of others. You can do it! There is nothing on this green Earth that you cannot accomplish if you're willing to dedicate hard work, discipline and delayed gratification to achieve it. You must be willing to forgive yourself for your imperfections and forgive those who may have mishandled you. Once you have accepted forgiveness for yourself and others, and you pursue your purpose with passion, the promise of that process is freedom! You simply have to realize that The Price of Freedom is service.

Chapter Seventeen

MAN IN THE MIRROR

EVERYONE says I'm the spitting image of my father—even though I'm still working on my beard. I thank God that I have my father's hustler's instinct. I'm not like most physicians who are complacent with being a doctor. I have worked hard to be a physician, chief medical examiner, and now author. My relationship with my father is better than I could have ever imagined. I have learned through forgiving him and knowing him I have more access to myself. What a blessing. Now, when I look at my dad in the mirror I give all thanks to God that He changed his ways...

1980
"Here's looking at you son."
-Dad

Roger A. Mitchell, Jr. MD

Dr. Roger Mitchell Jr. is board certified in Anatomic and Forensic Pathology by the American Board of Pathology. He is a Fellow with the American Society of Clinical Pathology (ASCP) and the National Association of Medical Examiners (NAME). Dr. Mitchell sits on national subcommittees for NAME including Education & Planning and Strategic Planning.

He is a graduate of Howard University, Washington DC, and UMDNJ-New Jersey Medical School, Newark, NJ. Dr. Mitchell is licensed to practice medicine in New Jersey and Washington DC. He has performed over 1300 autopsy examinations in his career and has testified as an expert on numerous cases.

He began the study of forensic science and violence prevention as a Forensic Biologist for the Federal Bureau of Investigation (FBI) – DNA Unit in January 1997 at the FBI Headquarters Building.

Dr. Mitchell served 4 years as the Assistant Deputy Chief Medical Examiner, in charge of Medicolegal Death Investigations, at the Harris County Institute of Forensic Sciences prior to serving 2 years as the Regional Medical Examiner for the Northern Regional Medical Examiner Office in Newark, NJ. Dr. Mitchell has served in large cities such as New York City, Houston, and Newark, NJ.

Dr. Mitchell has great interest in Violence as a public health issue. He believes the medical examiner serves a critical role in public health prevention initiatives and continues to be at the forefront of issues relating to Elder Abuse & Neglect and Youth Violence. He is recently published for his work on "Forensic Markers Associated with a History of Elder Mistreatment and Self Neglect" in the *Academic Forensic Pathology* journal.

He is also well versed in Mass Fatality Management and pledges his commitment to the preparedness of Washington DC.

Dr. Mitchell is no "new comer" to the District. In addition to receiving his undergraduate degree in biology from Howard University, Dr. Mitchell performed his pathology residency at George Washington University Hospital where he served as Chief Resident.

Dr. Roger A. Mitchell, Jr. is dedicated to the service of our community and is excited to serve our nation's capital as its next Chief Medical Examiner.

He is married to a DC native and has three wonderful children.

For more information log on to
www.freedomhasaprice.com

or for bookings email
info@freedomhasaprice.com

CPSIA information can be obtained at www.ICGtesting.com
Printed in the USA
BVOW08s1122080315

390773BV00011B/190/P